# WALKING
# *BARCELONA*

# WALKING
# BARCELONA

## THE BEST OF THE CITY

*Judy Thomson*

NATIONAL GEOGRAPHIC
Washington, D.C.

# WALKING
# BARCELONA

## CONTENTS

### PART 1

### PART 2

### PART 3

**Previous pages:
La Pedrera; left:
Santa Maria
del Mar; right:
Mirador de
Colom; above
right: fish at
L'Aquàrium;
bottom right:
Spanish artists
Miró, Picasso,
and Dalí**

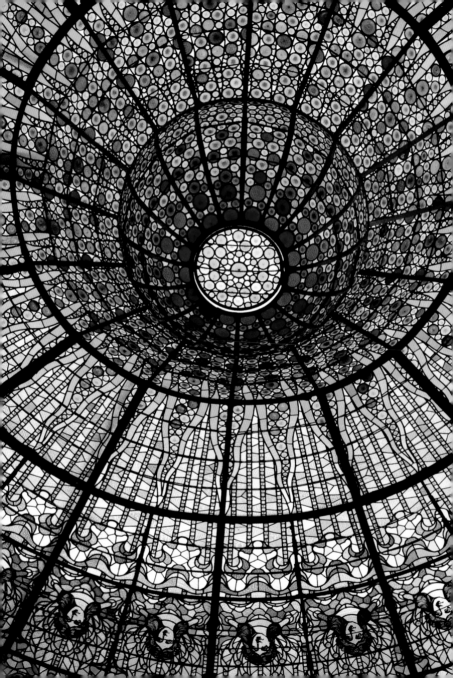

# Introduction

**W**hat could be more difficult for a young photographer who dreams of taking his camera to the remotest corners of the globe than for his first professional job to be to document his own city? Having since lived my dream of traveling the world as a photographer for National Geographic, I now see how much I owed my success in that first challenge to Barcelona itself, described by the writer Eduardo Mendoza, in the title of one of his novels, as *The City of Marvels.* At the time, I knew the Catalan capital as a colorful seaside metropolis punctuated by Modernist monuments, narrow medieval streets, lively marketplaces, and the world-famous Ramblas. As a photographer, I had to approach the city where I had been born and raised like a tourist searching for himself in a foreign land. Following a route mapped by instinct and emotion, I was seduced by its hidden beauty, its endless capacity to surprise.

**The stained-glass skylight over the auditorium at the Palau de la Música Catalana**

While Barcelona is rightfully distinguished by the legacy of artists such as Miró, Picasso, and Gaudí, I encourage you to venture beyond its most famous attractions: To follow the Passeig de Gràcia through the Plaça de Catalunya, past the towering statue of Columbus at the bottom of La Rambla, and into La Barceloneta, the bustling maritime neighborhood; to wind through the multicultural labyrinth of the Raval; or admire the meticulously planned elegance of the Eixample. Along the way, you will find the best of the classic Mediterranean lifestyle—and you might just find a bit of yourself, as well.

*Tino Soriano*
*National Geographic photographer*

# Visiting Barcelona

Barcelona is one of the liveliest and most rapidly changing cities in Europe. Situated between the sea and hills, with medieval streets and the latest architectural gems, Barcelona welcomes more than seven million visitors each year to enjoy beaches, culture, and a world-famous nightlife.

VISITING BARCELONA

## Barcelona in a Nutshell

The Mediterranean Sea laps the edge of the city on a series of newly created beaches and along the port. Inland, the hills of Montjuïc and Tibidabo provide splendid views across the city. This location brought the city prosperity in the Middle Ages when merchants built splendid palaces in narrow streets near the port, which now contain bars, shops, and museums. In the late 19th century, *modernista* architecture gave Barcelona some of its most famous sites, many built by Antoni Gaudí, from La Sagrada Família to the Park Güell and La Pedrera.

## Navigating Barcelona

The wide Avinguda (Avenue) Diagonal cuts across Barcelona, with the port, old town, and most of the main sites situated to the south, and La Sagrada

## Barcelona Day-by-Day

**Open every day** (with some exceptions for major public holidays) CaixaForum, Catedral, La Pedrera, La Sagrada Família, Mirador de Colom, L'Aquàrium, Casa Batlló, Palau de la Música Catalana, FC Barcelona Museum, Poble Espanyol, Fundació Mies van der Rohe, Park Güell.

**Monday** Most sites are closed except for above and MACBA, L'Auditori/Museu de la Música, Fundación Francisco Godia, Fundació Suñol. Many sites open if Monday is a public holiday.

**Tuesday** All sites open except MACBA, Museu de la Música, Fundación Francisco Godia.

**Wednesday** All sites open.

**Thursday** All sites open; also, opening day for new exhibitions—the public is often welcome.

**Friday** All sites open and best day for markets.

**Saturday** All sites open, but some shops close in the afternoon, especially in summer.

**Sunday** All sites open. Many museums are free on the first Sunday of the month. Municipal museums are free after 3 p.m. Maremàgnum shopping mall and Rambla del Raval market are open. Some traditional restaurants close in the evening.

**Fiestas with giant figures (*gegants*) reflect the party atmosphere the city's locals enjoy.**

Família, Park Güell, and smarter residential areas to the north. Two main roads, Rambla de Catalunya and Passeig de Gràcia, run from Diagonal to Plaça de Catalunya. From there, La Rambla leads to the port. There are official maps at the tourist information offices, main roads are clearly marked, and there are local maps near Metro stations.

Once you venture into the small streets of the old town—Barri Gòtic, La Ribera, and El Raval—the twists, turns, and inviting passageways will soon lure you into a maze where you may become lost, but that adds to the fun. The contrast between the old town and the more geometric layout of the 19th-century extension to the city, the Eixample, stands out on the map, and you can imagine the medieval walls that once surrounded the old town.

### The Rhythm of the City
Barcelona is a city for night owls, so you will need to adapt to local times. Breakfast is at the usual time, but lunch is not served until 2 p.m. and lasts until 4 p.m. Many shops and offices are closed during this time, but usually stay open until 8 p.m. or 9 p.m. Dinner starts at around 9 p.m. and may be served until midnight. Many clubs only open their doors after midnight.

# Using This Guide

Each tour—which might be only a walk, or might take advantage of the city's public transportation as well—is plotted on a map and has been planned to take into account opening hours and the times of day when sites are less crowded. Many end near restaurants or lively nightspots for evening activities.

### Whirlwind Tours

Whirlwind Tours are for people who have only a day or a weekend to spend in the city and want to be sure that they see the very best. Choose your tour based on your time and interests: One Day; Weekend (Day 1 & Day 2); For Fun; For Foodies; and With Kids (Day 1 & Day 2).

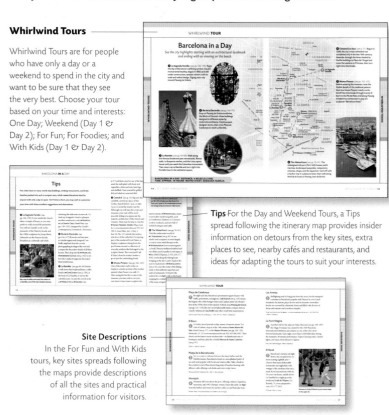

**Tips** For the Day and Weekend Tours, a Tips spread following the itinerary map provides insider information on detours from the key sites, extra places to see, nearby cafés and restaurants, and ideas for adapting the tours to suit your interests.

### Site Descriptions

In the For Fun and With Kids tours, key sites spreads following the maps provide descriptions of all the sites and practical information for visitors.

## Neighborhood Tours

The eight neighborhood tours each begin with an introduction, followed by an itinerary map highlighting the key sites that make up the tour and detailed key sites descriptions. Each tour is followed by an "in-depth" spread showcasing one major site along the route, a "distinctly" Barcelona spread providing background information on a quintessential element of that neighborhood, and a "best of" spread that groups sites thematically.

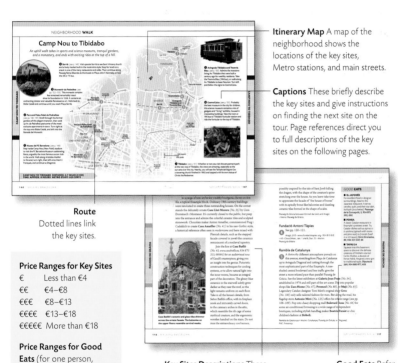

**Itinerary Map** A map of the neighborhood shows the locations of the key sites, Metro stations, and main streets.

**Captions** These briefly describe the key sites and give instructions on finding the next site on the tour. Page references direct you to full descriptions of the key sites on the following pages.

**Route**
Dotted lines link the key sites.

**Price Ranges for Key Sites**

| € | Less than €4 |
|---|---|
| €€ | €4–€8 |
| €€€ | €8–€13 |
| €€€€ | €13–€18 |
| €€€€€ | More than €18 |

**Price Ranges for Good Eats** (for one person, excluding drinks)

| € | Less than €15 |
|---|---|
| €€ | €15–€25 |
| €€€ | €25–€40 |
| €€€€ | €40–€60 |
| €€€€€ | More than €60 |

**Key Sites Descriptions** These provide a detailed description and highlights for each site, following the order on the map, plus its address, website, phone number, entrance fee, days closed, and nearest Metro station and bus stops.

**Good Eats** Refer to these lists—as well as Barcelona for Foodies (see pp. 28–31)—for a selection of cafés and restaurants.

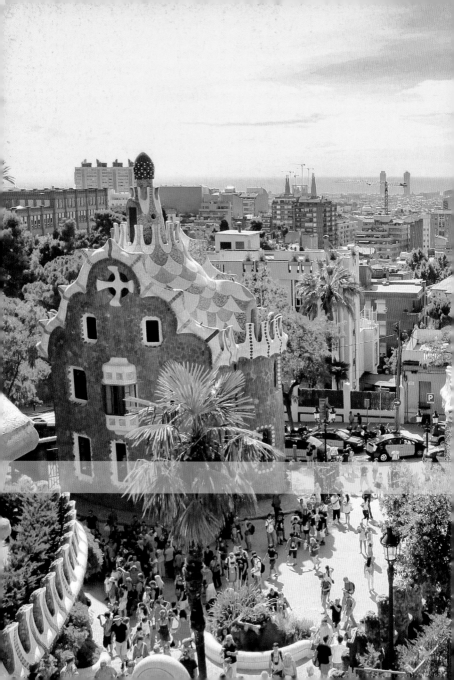

PART 1

# Whirlwind Tours

# Barcelona in a Day

*See the city highlights starting with an architectural landmark
and ending with an evening on the beach.*

❶ **La Sagrada Família** (see pp. 136–139) Begin
the day at Barcelona's defining symbol. Gaudí's
monumental basilica, begun in 1882 and still
under construction, amazes visitors with its
scale and radical design. Zigzag your way
toward Passeig de Gràcia.

❷ **Illa de la Discòrdia** (see pp. 116–117)
Stop on Passeig de Gràcia to admire
the Block of Discord—three buildings
designed in different styles by
*modernista* architects. Continue past
designer stores, then cross Plaça de
Catalunya to reach La Rambla.

❸ **La Rambla** (see pp. 60–69) Walk along
this famous boulevard past newsstands, flower
stalls, La Boqueria market, and the Liceu opera
house until you reach the Columbus monument.
Then return up La Rambla and turn right into
Portaferrissa to the cathedral square.

**BARCELONA IN A DAY  DISTANCE: 4 MILES (6.5 KM)
TIME: APPROX. 10 HOURS  METRO START: SAGRADA FAMÍLIA**

**4** **Catedral (La Seu)** (see p. 51)  Begun in 1298, the city's main cathedral was completed only in the late 19th century. Meander through the lanes shaded by Gothic buildings to Plaça de l'Àngel and cross Via Laietana to Princesa, then turn right onto Montcada.

**5** **Museu Picasso** (see pp. 102–105)  Before entering the museum, note the Gothic details of the medieval palaces that now house Picasso's early works. Stroll from Montcada through trendy El Born to the Pla de Palau and along Passeig d'Isabel II to Lichtenstein's pop-art sculpture "Barcelona Head."

**6** **The Waterfront** (see pp. 76–91)  The redesigned old port (Port Vell) houses yacht marinas, landscaped quaysides, restaurants, cinemas, shops, and the aquarium. Cool off with a harbor trip in a pleasure boat, then walk along Moll de la Fusta to Passeig Joan de Borbó.

# Tips

Few cities have so many world-class buildings, striking monuments, and lively beaches packed into such a compact area, which makes Barcelona ideal for anyone with only a day to spare. Yet if time is short, you may wish to customize your time with these excellent suggestions and alternatives.

**WHIRLWIND TOURS**

❶ **La Sagrada Família** (see pp. 136–139) A tour inside the church takes a couple of hours, so you may prefer to walk around the perimeter. You will see Gaudí's work on the pinnacles of the Nativity facade and the 1980s sculptures by Josep María Subirachs on the Passion facade. Breakfast at a sidewalk café while

Sip a cup of coffee and watch the action on La Rambla, one of the city's busiest avenues.

admiring the elaborate stonework. Or dash up Avinguda Gaudí to glimpse another *modernista* work, ■ **HOSPITAL DE LA SANTA CREU I SANT PAU** (see pp. 130–131), designed by Gaudí's contemporary, Domènech i Montaner.

❷ **Illa de la Discòrdia** (see pp. 116–117) If you do not have time to visit the ingeniously designed Casa Batlló, step back from the crowds photographing its dragon-like roof and compare the decorative details of all three houses. Then drop into the ■ **MUSEU DEL MODERNISME CATALÀ** (see p. 143) to see how the Catalan bourgeoisie decorated their lavish homes.

❸ **La Rambla** (see pp. 60–69) Before a walk down this boulevard have a coffee break in ■ **CAFÉ ZURICH** (see p. 124), at the head of La Rambla, to survey the colorful scene. Or, join the crowds as far as ■ **MERCAT DE LA BOQUERIA** (see

p. 67) and find a stool at one of the bars amid the stalls piled with fruits and vegetables, olives and nuts, ham legs and shellfish. Treat yourself to grilled fish and salad or a seasonal dish.

**❹ Catedral** (see p. 51) Slip into the candlelit, cavernous space of this Gothic church before 1 p.m. or after 5 p.m. to avoid the tourist visit fee. Although you will miss the crypt and museum, your visit will be more peaceful, letting you appreciate the majestic architecture of the church and cloisters. There may be time to visit the ■ **MUSEU FREDERIC MARÉS** (*Plaça Sant Iu, 5, www.museumares.bcn.cat, 932 563 500, €, closed Mon., Jan. 1, May 1, June 24, Dec. 25*) outside the eastern side door of the cathedral. Occupying part of the medieval Royal Palace, it displays sculptures dating from the pre-Roman era and a collection of everyday artifacts that belonged to the sculptor Marès. The courtyard Cafè d'Estiu (closed in winter) makes a good spot for a refreshing break.

**❺ Museu Picasso** (see pp. 102–105) One of the artist's early works on display is a tender portrait of his mother painted when Picasso was only 15. After seeing the first few rooms in the museum, you may wish to cut your visit short to leave time to explore the

## CUSTOMIZING **YOUR DAY**

Pop into the Palau de la Virreina (see p. 66) next to La Boqueria market for leaflets about festivals, concerts, and other cultural activities in the city. You can even buy tickets for events here. A concert at the Palau de la Música Catalana (see pp. 96–97) will give you the chance to feast your eyes on this *modernista* concert hall designed by Domènech i Montaner.

narrow streets off ■ **MONTCADA,** many named after medieval guilds, such as Sombrerers (hatters) or Cotoners (cotton workers), and now full of stylish boutiques and cafés.

**❻ The Waterfront** (see pp. 76–91) Visit the underwater world of ■ **L'AQUÀRIUM** (see p. 81) to see sharks and octopuses at arm's length, or enjoy some retail therapy in the ■ **MAREMAGNUM** (*www.maremagnum .es*) mall. Then try traditional seafood and rice dishes, such as paella or *arròs negre,* at ■ **ELX** (*Moll d'Espanya, 5, 932 258 117, €€€*), overlooking the fishing boats bringing in the day's catch. Explore the narrow backstreets of ■ **BARCELONETA** (see p. 35), once the center of the fishing trade, to find authentic tapas bars and seafood restaurants. Or head to the seafront for a twilight walk on the beach, stopping for cocktails in the sand at one of the many *xiringuitos* (beach bars).

# Barcelona in a Weekend

*The first day of your tour takes you through atmospheric squares,
up to museums on a hill, and by cable car to the port.*

**❸ Fundació Joan Miró** (see p. 166) See a world-class collection of Miró's work in this custom-built museum flooded with light. Walk along Avinguda de l'Estadi, and opposite the Picornell swimming pool, take the path and escalator to the Palau Nacional.

**❹ Museu Nacional** (see pp. 168–169) This monumental building from the 1929 International Exhibition houses 1,000 years of Catalan art and offers great views of the city. Return to the Picornell swimming pool, take bus 150 to Plaça de Carlos Ibáñez, and catch the cable car.

**❷ Palau Güell** (see pp. 70–71) A young Gaudí designed this town house for his patron, industrialist Eusebi Güell, in 1885. Check out its austere facade from across the street, then see the wealth of details inside. Walk to the Paral·lel Metro to catch the funicular up to Montjuïc.

| 0 | 1 kilometer |
| 0 | 1/2 mile |

Rocafort · Urgell
Espanya · GRAN VIA DE LES CORTS CATALAN
CaixaForum · Sant Antoni
La Font Màgica · Mercat de Sant Antoni
Poble Espanyol · Pavelló Mies van der Rohe · Poble Sec
**❹ Museu Nacional**
ANELLA OLÍMPICA · Sant Pau del Camp
Estadi Olímpic · **Fundació ❸ Joan Miró**
Avinguda de Miramar · Paral·lel
MONTJUÏC · **Cable ca Barcelor**
Castell de Montjuïc · Mirador · Miramar · **❺**
Museu Militar · Castell de Montjuïc
Dàrsena Sant Bert

**❺ Cable car to Barceloneta** (see p. 84) Glide over the harbor in a cable car giving a bird's-eye view of the huge port below and the city stretching back to Tibidabo in the Collserola hills. You will arrive at the Torre de Sant Sebastià and emerge near the beaches.

**BARCELONA IN A WEEKEND DAY 1  DISTANCE: 3.4 MILES (5.5 KM)
TIME: APPROX. 9 HOURS  METRO START: LICEU**

**8 Plaça Reial** (see p. 53) The infinite choice of bars and restaurants nestling in the arches of this handsome 19th-century square makes it the perfect place to unwind after a long day's outing.

**1 Mercat de la Boqueria** (see pp. 16–17, 67) Breakfast amid stallholders setting up displays of fresh produce in the city's main market. Try baby squid and poached eggs with cava, then continue down La Rambla to Nou de la Rambla.

**7 Plaça de Sant Jaume** (see p. 50) This cobbled square, once the Roman forum, houses the Palau de la Generalitat, seat of the Catalan government, and the Casa de la Ciutat, where the City Council meets. Take Ferran and turn into Plaça Reial.

**6 The Waterfront** (see pp. 76–91) Take a stroll along the city's 3 miles (4.8 km) of beaches (all with showers), then follow the edge of the port past palm trees and skateboarders to Moll de la Fusta, cross over Passeig de Colom, and go up Regomir.

# Barcelona in a Weekend

*Look inside magnificent buildings and museums on your second day,
and take time out in two city parks.*

**❶ Park Güell**
(see pp. 70–71, 131–133)
Make an early start
to avoid the crowds
who flock to Gaudí's
charming park sculpted
out of the hillside. Take
the Metro to Sagrada
Família, changing lines
at Diagonal.

**❷ La Sagrada Família** (see pp. 136–139) **Buy tickets
online ahead of time for quick entry into Gaudí's
masterpiece. Walk along Provença to admire the
intricate *modernista* details of doorways, balconies, and
rooftops until you reach La Pedrera, on the corner of
Passeig de Gràcia.**

L'ESQUERRA
DE L'EIXAMPL

Urgell

Universitat

Sant
Antoni

MACBA
**EL RAVA**

Mercat de
la Boqueria

Lice

Gran Teatre
del Lice

Palau Güell

Drassanes

Mirador
de Colom

Jaume

**❸ La Pedrera (Casa Milà)**
(see pp. 118–119) **Gaudí's
extraordinary apartment
house weaves its way around
the corner, an embodiment
of this visionary architect's
belief in organic forms. Take
the Metro to Catalunya then
walk down Portal de l'Àngel.**

**BARCELONA IN A WEEKEND DAY 2   DISTANCE: 3.1 MILES (5 KM)
TIME: APPROX. 11 HOURS   METRO START: LESSEPS**

WHIRLWIND TOURS

**0** | **1 kilometer**
**0** | **1/2 mile**

**Park Güell**
**1**

Casa Museu Gaudí

**EL CARMEL**

Lesseps

Casa Vicenç

Fontana

**GRÀCIA**

Joanic

Alfons X

Hospital de la Santa Creu i Sant Pau

Hotel Casa Fuster

**LA SAGRADA FAMÍLIA**

Hospital de Sant Pau

**La Pedrera (Casa Milà)**
**3**

Verdaguer

Sagrada Família

**La Sagrada Família**
**2**

Passeig de Gràcia

Encants

GRÀCIA

Girona

**L'EIXAMPLE**

Tetuan

Monumental

GRAN VIA DE LES CORTS CATALANES

Glòries

Urquinaona

L'Auditori & Museu de la Música

Palau de la Música Catalana

Arc de Triomf

Marina

**Catedral (La Seu)**

**LA RIBERA**

**4**

Mercat de Santa Caterina

JHBA Plaça el Rei

**5**

**Museu Picasso**
**6**

Jaume I

**7**

**8** **Parc de la Ciutadella**

Tica de Mercè

Santa Maria del Mar

**Born Centre Cultural**

Parlament de Catalunya

Barceloneta

Ciutadella Vila Olímpica

RT VELL

L'Aquàrium

Museu d'Història de Catalunya

**LA BARCELONETA**

emàgnum

Platja de la Barceloneta

Platja de Somorrostro

**❹ Catedral (La Seu)** (see p. 51) The city's main cathedral is framed by the remains of Roman watchtowers and heavy stone walls. Take Comtes, the narrow street along the side of the cathedral, and turn left after the Palau del Lloctinent.

**❺ MUHBA Plaça del Rei** (see pp. 54–55) Absorb the atmosphere of this medieval square bordered by the walls of the former Royal Palace. Then visit MUHBA (History Museum of Barcelona) housed in the palace. Go down Llibreteria, cross Via Laietana, and take Princesa as far as Montcada.

**❻ Museu Picasso** (see pp. 102–105) The early work of one of the 20th century's greatest artists are housed in mansions built in Catalonia's medieval heyday. Walk down Montcada and turn left into Passeig del Born.

**❼ Born Centre Cultural** (see p. 100) Located in an old wrought-iron market building, this cultural center displays the remains of the 18th-century city found underneath it. Walk through the building and cross Passeig de Picasso.

**❽ Parc de la Ciutadella** (see pp. 100–101) In 1714, Spanish troops built a citadel here. Later, the area became a park, which also houses the Catalan parliament and the zoo; it is perfect for a twilight walk.

# Tips

Two days in Barcelona will give you enough time to see the city's main sights. The cross-references in the text below will guide you to detailed information elsewhere in the book. These tips offer you some detours to other attractions and suggest alternatives to suit your interests and customize your day.

WHIRLWIND TOURS

## DAY 1

❶ **Mercat de la Boqueria** (see pp. 16–17, 67) The lanes of the market are busy in the morning as stallholders prepare displays of fresh produce. For a quieter place to breakfast, leave by the rear entrance to find the ■ **ANTIC HOSPITAL DE LA SANTA CREU** (see p. 66). Discover the peaceful courtyard of a medieval hospital complex and eat at the restaurant, El Jardí (*Hospital, 56, 932 853 834*).

**La Boqueria draws crowds of food lovers.**

❸ **Fundació Joan Miró** (see p. 166) If you prefer sport to art, skip one of the museums and take a closer look at the ■ **OLYMPIC STADIUM,** ■ **PALAU SANT JORDI** (see p. 165), and ■ **MUSEU OLÍMPIC I DE L'ESPORT** (*Avinguda de l'Estadi, 60, www.museuolimpicbcn.cat, €€, closed Mon., Jan. 1, May 1, Dec. 25–26*). Walk through some of this hill's gardens on your way to the cable car, not missing the ■ **PISCINA MUNICIPAL DE MONTJUÏC** (see p. 172), where the 1992 Olympics diving event took place.

❼ **Plaça de Sant Jaume** (see p. 50) If you have time, take in the charms of the area nearby. ■ **CALL,** the main street of the medieval Jewish quarter (see p. 49), leads to Banys Nous. Stop at No. 8 for a sugar boost in the family-run *xurreria* (doughnut shop), then find ■ **PLAÇA DE SANT JOSEP ORIOL** (see p. 49), with its weekend art market, and adjacent ■ Plaça del Pi (see pp. 48–49)dominated by ■ Santa Maria del Pi (see p. 57), a sturdy Gothic church. These are two of the most atmospheric squares in the old town.

## DAY 2

**❷ La Sagrada Família** (see pp. 136–139) If you prefer a walk to the church visit, explore the Gràcia neighborhood near Park Güell. It retains the atmosphere of the village it once was, characterized by narrow streets with traditional and trendy shops, and dotted with squares full of terrace cafés and bars.

**❸ La Pedrera (Casa Milà)** (see pp. 118–119) Observe the building from across the street for a good view of its undulating facade and "witch-scarer" chimneys. Free temporary exhibitions give a glimpse of some interior details. Then window-shop your way down chic ■ Passeig de Gràcia (see pp. 115–126), pausing to take in the dazzling facades of the three *modernista* houses in the ■ Illa de la Discòrdia (see pp. 116–117).

**❻ Museu Picasso** (see pp. 102–105) After 3 p.m. on Sundays there is no entrance charge, so you may get in for free, but lines can be long. Even if you opt not to visit, take time to look at the facades of the magnificent mansions on this street. Then walk up Sombrerers

### CUSTOMIZING **YOUR DAY**

If shopping is high on your list, bear in mind that most shops close on Sunday. Larger stores stay open until 9 p.m., so make shopping part of your Saturday tour. Hop up to Passeig de Gràcia on the Metro from Barceloneta or Drassanes for sophisticated designer shopping. Or explore the Born boutiques (see p. 99) or the quirky shops in Avinyó and Banys Nous, near Plaça Sant Jaume. On Sunday the Maremàgnum shops *(until 10 p.m. every day)* and the market in Rambla del Raval (see p. 69) are open.

to the church of ■ Santa Maria del Mar (see pp. 98–99), perhaps the most beautiful example of Catalan Gothic architecture (see pp. 56–57) in the city and a serene space for meditation.

**❽ Parc de la Ciutadella** (see pp. 100–101) If you have kids with you, be sure to get to the park in time to visit the zoo (see p. 101), perhaps visiting the Born Centre Cultural afterward. You can rent bikes nearby *(Passeig de Picasso, 40),* or rent rowboats on the park's lake. Return to El Born's lanes for cocktails, tapas, or elegant dining at Senyor Parellada *Argentería, 37, www.senyorparellada.com, 933 105 094, €€€),* a restaurant serving new versions of traditional Catalan dishes in charming surroundings.

# Barcelona for Fun

*Some chic shopping, a little sea and sand, a couple of sky-high rides, and a cup of hot chocolate are just a few highlights of this diverse day in Barcelona.*

**WHIRLWIND TOURS**

**7** **El Raval** (see pp. 27, 60–75) Grab dinner, drinks, and a little music in El Raval, the hub of Barcelona's eclectic nightlife scene. Past midnight, stroll down La Rambla to the moody Gòtic area and glide into Café de l'Òpera for a hot chocolate.

**6** **La Font Màgica** (see pp. 27, 75) Built in 1929, this is Barcelona's largest public fountain. Although spectacular by day, the magic doesn't happen until after dark when the fountain erupts with music, light, and dancing water. Retrace your steps to Plaça d'Espanya and hop Metro Line 1 to Universitat station.

**5** **Las Arenas** (see pp. 27, 162) This historic bullring has become a modern shopping mall with a flying-saucer-like dome above a mélange of boutiques, cafés, and entertainment outlets. Amble down Avinguda de la Reina Maria Cristina to the fountain.

Map labels:
Entença
AVINGUDA DE R
Tarragona
**5** **Las Arenas** Rocafort
Espanya GRAN VIA DE
Merca Sant An
Poble Sec
**6** La Font Màgica
Museu Nacional
ANELLA OLÍMPICA
Fundació Joan Miró
Estadi Olímpic
Avinguda de Miramar
**MONTJUÏC** Montjuïc
CEMENTIRI DEL SUD-OEST
Castell de Montjuïc
**4** Mirador Mira
Castell de Montjuïc
Museu Militar
RONDA DEL LITORAL
Dàrsena del Morrot
Moll del Sud
Moll per a Petrolers
0 1 kilometer
0 1/2 mile

**BARCELONA FOR FUN DISTANCE: 6.1 MILES (9.8 KM)**
**TIME: 11–12 HOURS METRO START: PLAÇA DE CATALUNYA**

**❶ Plaça de Catalunya** (see pp. 26, 114–115)
Grab an outdoor table at Café Zurich. Order
breakfast and watch the crowds swirling through
the Plaça de Catalunya at the top of La Rambla.
Afterward browse the Passeig de Gràcia, Spain's
chicest shopping street. Take Portal de l'Àngel
around the cathedral to El Born.

**❷ El Born** (see pp. 26, 99)  Get medieval in El
Born, an ancient barrio spangled with Gothic
architecture and narrow streets. Shopping
ranges from funky one-off fashion boutiques
to the sprawling Mercat de Santa Caterina.
After visiting the Museu Picasso, walk Passeig
de Joan de Borbó to the sea.

**❸ Platja de la Barceloneta** (see p. 26)
Catch some rays on Barceloneta beach, a
crescent of golden sand between the big
blue sail (W Hotel) and the giant fish (Frank
Gehry's "Peix d'Or"). Head to the iron Torre
de Sant Sebastià to catch the cable car.

**❹ Montjuïc** (see pp. 26, 158–173)  Snatch a bird's-
eye view of the port and its giant cruise ships from
one of the red cable cars that glide between the
beach and Montjuïc hill. Stroll the lofty gardens
and then ride the cable car and funicular railroad
combination to Paral·lel station; follow the broad
avenue of the same name due west.

## Plaça de Catalunya

**1** By night and day, Barcelona's preeminent square buzzes with traffic, pedestrians, and pigeons. **Café Zurich** (see p. 124) retains the bygone vibe of the foreign writers and Catalan artists who flocked here in the 1930s when it first opened. A block away, **Passeig de Gràcia** (see pp. 115–116), the city's most fashionable street, contains Antoni Gaudí's whimsical **Casa Batlló** and other *modernista* masterpieces.

Café Zurich, Plaça de Catalunya, 1 • 933 179 153 • Metro: Catalunya

## El Born

**2** A Gothic mood prevails in this warren of narrow streets. For a hit of culture, stop in at the 14th-century **Santa Maria del Mar** church (see p. 57), or the **Museu Picasso** (see pp. 102–105; *Montcada, 15–23, www.museupicasso.bcn.cat, 932 563 000, €€€*). Then check out the barrio's more modern side—its flamboyant mix of boutiques and bars, plus the colorful **Mercat de Santa Caterina** (see p. 97).

El Born • Metro: Jaume I

## Platja de la Barceloneta

**3** Set on a narrow isthmus between the inner harbor and the Mediterranean, Barceloneta beach is a sun-splashed patch of sea and sand popular with locals and visitors alike. Take a break at this southern end of Barcelona's long strip of beaches buzzing with alfresco cafés offering cool drinks and even cooler views.

Passeig Marítim Barceloneta • Metro: Barceloneta

## Montjuïc

**4** Montjuïc hill rises above the port, offering a mixture of gardens, museums, and 1992 Olympic venues. Enjoy the cable car flight from the harbor and return by another cable car and funicular train.

Metro: Paral·lel and funicular and telefèric de Montjuïc

## Las Arenas

**5** Bullfighting may be long gone from the arena, but the stampede continues at Barcelona's popular mall. Bizarre by even Gaudí standards, the historic *plaza de toros* and its dramatic *neomudéjar* facade are crowned by a futuristic dome and filled with all sorts of shops and eateries and a modern cineplex.

Gran Via de les Corts Catalanes • www.arenasdebarcelona.com • 932 890 244
• Metro: Espanya

## La Font Màgica

**6** A perfect foil for the adjacent Palau Nacional (see pp. 168–169) the Magic Fountain was created for the 1929 Barcelona International Exhibition and endures as one of the city's most beloved landmarks. Each night, more than 4,500 bulbs blaze during the fountain's 30-minute performance. Expect dancing water, colored lights, and music from Mozart to Queen.

Plaça de Carles Buïgas • Metro: Espanya

## El Raval

**7** Barcelona's onetime red-light district has morphed into its most exciting nightlife area— a barrio that mixes fashionable restaurants and nightclubs with vestiges of the seediness that once made Raval synonymous with sin. On your way home, ramble down La Rambla for a nightcap at the traditional **Café de l'Òpera** (*La Rambla, 74, www.cafeoperabcn .com, 933 177 585*).

El Raval • Metro: Liceu

**Dancers in lively El Raval try out some steps in the open air.**

# Barcelona for Foodies

*A paradise for food aficionados, the city offers classic restaurants and contemporary eateries, as well as markets brimming with produce and stores selling designer kitchenware.*

**7 Vinçon** (see p. 31) Don't miss this cathedral of design, specializing in tempting kitchenware for gourmet cooks. Continue to Rosselló.

**6 Casa Calvet** (see p. 31) Pick up some culture and delicious Brescó chocolate in this Gaudí-designed house. Walk a couple of blocks and turn right onto Passeig de Gràcia.

**5 Vila Viniteca** (see p. 31) Located in a medieval building, this shop stocks a huge range of wines. Wander through La Ribera until it meets Eixample, take Bruc, and turn left onto Casp.

**8 Roca Moo** (see p. 31) Dinner in a restaurant managed by the Roca brothers, ranked among the world's top chefs, makes a fitting climax to a gourmet day.

**1 Granja Viader** (see p. 30) Start at this family-run milk bar where the popular chocolate drink *Cacaolat* was invented. Continue down Xuclà to Carme, turn right, then left to find the side entrance to La Boqueria.

**2 Mercat de la Boqueria** (see pp. 30, 67) See the city's most popular market as it comes to life and sample dishes at market bars, such as El Quim. Cross La Rambla and walk through Barri Gòtic, cross Via Laietana, onto Princesa, then Montcada.

**4 Restaurant 7 Portes** (see pp. 30–31) Eat lunch in one of the city's oldest restaurants, opposite the Llotja, the former stock exchange. Return to the Llotja and take Canvis Vells, then turn left onto Agullers.

**3 El Xampanyet** (see p. 30) To drink an *aperitivo* at this bar, dating from 1929, you may have to fight for room. Cross Passeig del Born to Pla de Palau.

**BARCELONA FOR FOODIES  DISTANCE: 2.5 MILES (4 KM)
TIME: APPROX. 9 HOURS  METRO START: CATALUNYA**

### Granja Viader

**1** Track down the oldest milk bar in town on a narrow street parallel to La Rambla, for a *cafè amb llet* (milky coffee) and a *melindro* (sponge finger). Or try their famous *xocolata desfeta* (syrupy thick hot chocolate); topped with cream it becomes a *suís*.

Xuclà, 4–6 • 933 183 486 • Closed lunchtimes and Sun. • Metro: Catalunya

### Mercat de la Boqueria

**2** The side entrance to this mecca for food lovers takes you to the local farmers' stalls piled high with seasonal produce—an area most visitors miss (see p. 67). Join cooking writer Sophie Ruggles (*www.sophieruggles.com*) for an insider's market tour or take a class to learn to make local dishes, such as paella; book in advance.

La Rambla, 91 • www.boqueria.info • 933 182 584 • Closed Sun. and public holidays • Metro: Liceu

**Pretty ceramic tiles line the walls of the famous and historic bar, El Xampanyet.**

### El Xampanyet

**3** The house *cava* and local anchovies spiked with vinegar are the signature *aperitivo* of this tiny bar. Charming hosts also serve a *vermut*, red vermouth with a squirt of soda water, a favorite prelunch drink best with olives.

Montcada, 22 • 933 197 003 • Closed Sun. p.m.– Mon., and Aug. • Metro: Jaume I

### Restaurant 7 Portes

**4** Since 1836, this classic Barcelona restaurant has welcomed generations of Catalans to enjoy their specialty rice dishes, such as *arròs caldós,* a moist seafood paella, or roast shoulder of goat. On the weekend, eat on the terrace under the arches of this handsome restaurant.

Passeig Isabel II, 14 • www.7portes.com • 933 193 033 • Metro: Barceloneta

## Vila Viniteca

**5** Be guided by experts in this family-run business to find unusual, Catalan wines, or book ahead for a tasting conducted in English. The neighboring gourmet shop offers a range of Spanish delicacies.

Agullers, 7&9 • www.vilaviniteca.es • 902 327 777 • Closed Sun., and Sat. p.m. in July and Aug. • Metro: Jaume I

## Casa Calvet

**6** The top-echelon Casa Calvet restaurant serves Catalan dishes in historic surroundings. Visit the adjoining **Chocolates Brescó,** a famed master chocolate maker, to buy a bar of 99 percent cacao chocolate or sample a hot chocolate or milkshake.

Casp, 48 • www.chocolatesbresco.com • 974 543 008 • Closed Sun. • Metro: Urquinaona

## Vinçon

**7** Browse this huge store for the latest kitchen ideas from designers such as Luki Huber, who worked on culinary projects with the former Barcelona restaurant elBulli. See the original decor on the first floor, once home to *modernista* painter, Ramon Casas.

Passeig de Gràcia, 96 • www.vincon.com • 932 156 050 • Closed Sun. • Metro: Diagonal

## Roca Moo

**8** Treat yourself to the modern gourmet Catalan food that has won awards for the Roca brothers at this hotel restaurant. The contemporary open-plan space means you can watch the dishes being prepared. For the complete experience, the Joan Roca tasting menu offers eight dishes, ranging from seabass with truffles and artichokes to pear and tarragon, with matching wines.

Rosselló, 265 • www.hotelomm.es • 934 454 000 • Closed Sun. and Mon. • Metro: Diagonal

# Barcelona in a Weekend with Kids

*Animals and the great outdoors, chocolate and ice cream, infuse your first family day in Barcelona with a sense of adventure and good taste.*

❹ **Mirador de Colom** (see pp. 35, 83) Stroll along the harbor to the column in honor of Christopher Columbus's first voyage to the New World in 1492. Take the elevator to a lookout point at the top of the column for views in all directions.

❸ **Museu de la Xocolata** (see pp. 35, 142) Chocolate tasting, chocolate art, and a chance to submerge your hands in liquid chocolate make this museum a treat. Follow Carrer del Comerç, and then go right onto Passeig d'Isabel II to reach the harbor.

0   1 kilome
0   1/2 mile

Urgell

GRAN VIA DE LES CORTS CATALANES
Universitat
Sant Antoni   Catalunya
CCCB
Poble Sec   MACBA
**EL RAVAL**   **BARR**
  **GÒTIC**
Antic Hospital de la Santa Creu   Palau de la Virreina
Mercat de la Boqueria   Catedral
Sant Pau del Camp   Liceu
  MUH
AVINGUDA DEL PARAL·LEL
Avinguda de Miramar   Palau Güell   Jau
  Porta del Mar
Paral·lel   Drassanes
Museu Marítim de Barcelona
Mirador   **Mirador de Colom** ❹   Basíli La M
Miramar   **Golondrinas** ❺   **PORT V**
  L'Aquàri
Jaume I
Maremàgnum
Dàrsena de Sant Bertran   Sant Sebas

❺ **Golondrinas** (see pp. 35, 82) Cruise the port on a vintage vessel, or venture into the Mediterranean on one of the modern boats of the Golondrinas armada. Hail a taxi at the wharf and head for the beach.

**BARCELONA WITH KIDS DAY 1  DISTANCE: 3.9 MILES (6.3 KM)
TIME: APPROX. 9 HOURS  METRO START: ARC DE TRIOMF**

**❷ Barcelona Zoo** (see pp. 34–35, 101) Sprawling across the park, Barcelona's own menagerie is one of Europe's oldest. Among its highlights are the gorilla habitat and the Komodo dragons. Cross Passeig de Picasso and walk down Carrer de la Princesa.

**❶ Parc de la Ciutadella** (see pp. 34, 100–101) Start the day with a visit to Barcelona's oldest park. Pose for family photographs with the mythological creatures around the extravagant Cascada, a huge waterfall.

**❻ The Beach** (see pp. 35, 90–91) Spend the rest of the afternoon on one of Barcelona's popular beaches, framed by the huge blue W Hotel and Frank Gehry's giant fish sculpture, "Peix" ("Fish").

Rent a rowboat on Parc de la Ciutadella's large artificial lake, the Estany.

## Parc de la Ciutadella

**1** A breath of fresh air on the edge of the crowded old town, Parc de la Ciutadella offers a chance to go hiking, biking, and boating. Start your day with a boat ride on the lake beside the **Cascada** waterfall, which Gaudí helped to design. Breakfast in the open air at the nearby café, before walking through the park to the zoo.

Entrances on Passeig de Picasso and Passeig de Pujades • Metro: Arc de Triomf, Barceloneta, or Jaume I

## Barcelona Zoo

**2** From gorillas and orangutans to Barbary apes and putty-nosed monkeys, primates are the specialty of this captivating city zoo, showcasing about 400 species from around the globe. Dolphin and sea lion shows are staged in the Aquarama. As well as having a petting zoo for small children, the zoo holds special activities for kids and families most weekends that offer an insight into the lives of animals.

Passeig de Picasso, Parc de la Ciutadella • www.zoobarcelona.cat • 902 457 545 • €€€€ • Metro: Arc de Triomf, Barceloneta, or Jaume I

## Museu de la Xocolata

**3** How sweet it is! Barcelona's love of chocolate is the focus of this scrumptious museum where kids can taste, smell, make, and even paint with the delicious brown concoction. The museum's gallery contains miniature versions of **La Sagrada Família** and other Barcelona landmarks rendered in chocolate.

Carrer del Comerç 36 • www.museuxocolata.cat • 932 687 878 • € • Closed Jan. 1, 6, May 1, Dec. 25, 26 • Metro: Jaume I or Arc de Triomf

## Mirador de Colom

**4** Kids will enjoy looking out to sea from the dizzying heights of the Columbus Monument viewing platform. Back down below they may scramble over the giant lions guarding the monument.

Plaça Portal de la Pau • www.barcelonaturisme.com • 932 853 834 • € • Closed Jan. 1, Dec. 25 • Metro: Drassanes

## Golondrinas

**5** Classic boats cruise the port in 35 minutes; a catamaran takes you out to sea on a 90-minute trip. During the summer you can cruise between the Columbus Monument and the beaches.

Moll de Drassanes • www.lasgolondrinas.com • 934 423 106 • Port trip €€, Coast trip €€€ • Closed Jan. 1, Dec. 25 • Metro: Drassanes

## The Beach

**6** Barcelona's beaches stretch in a sandy arc from **Port Vell** and **Barceloneta** to the Fòrum. Platja de la Barceloneta is close to the center and one of the most family friendly.

Metro: Barceloneta

# Barcelona in a Weekend with Kids

*Take to some of the high points around Barcelona on your second day in the city and enjoy a walk through a jungle, a tour around Spain, and a spin on the Big Wheel.*

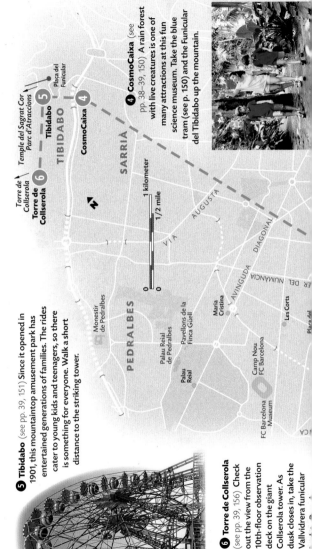

**5** **Tibidabo** (see pp. 39, 151) Since it opened in 1901, this mountaintop amusement park has entertained generations of families. The rides cater to young kids and teenagers, so there is something for everyone. Walk a short distance to the striking tower.

**6** **Torre de Collserola** (see pp. 39, 156) Check out the view from the 10th-floor observation deck on the giant Collserola tower. As dusk closes in, take the Vallvidrera funicular

**4** **CosmoCaixa** (see pp. 38–39, 150) A rain forest with live creatures is one of many attractions at this fun science museum. Take the blue funicular tram (see p. 150) and the Funicular del Tibidabo up the mountain.

Torre de Collserola
**Torre de Collserola**

Temple del Sagrat Cor
Parc d'Atraccions

**6**

Plaça del Funicular

**TIBIDABO**

**Tibidabo** **5**

**CosmoCaixa** **4**

**SARRIÀ**

Monestir de Pedralbes

**PEDRALBES**

Palau Reial de Pedralbes

Palau Reial

Pavellons de la Finca Güell

Maria Cristina

Camp Nou FC Barcelona

FC Barcelona Museum

Les Corts

VIA AUGUSTA

AVINGUDA DIAGONAL

ER DEL NUMÀNCIA

N

0            1 kilometer
0        1/2 mile

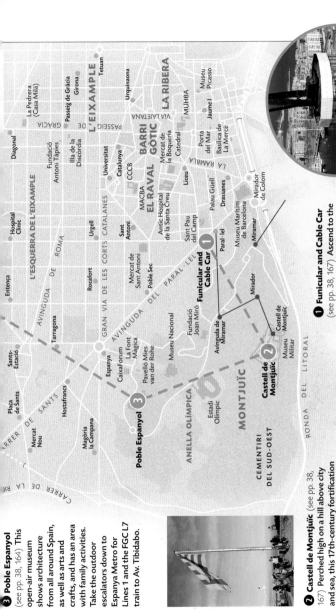

### 3 Poble Espanyol

(see pp. 38, 164) This open-air museum shows architecture from all around Spain, as well as arts and crafts, and has an area with family activities. Take the outdoor escalators down to Espanya Metro for Lines 1 and the FGC L7 train to Av. Tibidabo.

### 2 Castell de Montjuïc (see pp. 38,

167) Perched high on a hill above city and sea, this 17th-century fortification exudes a deep sense of history and the ghosts of those who perished within. Take Bus 150 to Poble Espanyol.

### 1 Funicular and Cable Car

(see pp. 38, 167) Ascend to the top of Montjuïc Hill by funicular railroad and cable car, starting from Paral·lel Metro station.

**BARCELONA WITH KIDS DAY 2 DISTANCE: 11 MILES (17.7 KM)**
**TIME: APPROX. 9 HOURS METRO START: PARAL·LEL**

### Funicular and Cable Car

**1** Start the day with a ride on the funicular railroad and cable car combination up the north side of Montjuïc hill. Most of the funicular runs underground, but kids will enjoy looking across the harbor and city center as they are swept into the air in these glass-sided cable cars.

Avinguda del Paral·lel • www.tmb.cat • € • Metro: Paral·lel

### Castell de Montjuïc

**2** Dating from the 1600s, this massive star-shaped fortress saw military action for many years before becoming an infamous prison. Kids will love the grizzly history of the castle, site of torture and executions. See the cannon that were meant to protect the city from invasion from the sea but were sometimes turned against it.

Carretera de Montjuïc • www.bcn.cat • 933 298 653 • Metro: Paral·lel

### Poble Espanyol

**3** Take a tour of Spain at this attraction on Montjuïc hill. Watch craftspeople at work in buildings representing the architecture of 15 regions, or just enjoy the games and shows. Stop for lunch at one of the many eateries, such as La Freiduría Tío Pepe *(Arcos, 9),* where you can sample a taste of southern Spain. They serve typical tapas including fried fish and *calamares a la romana* (squid), which are usually a hit with kids.

Avinguda de Francesc Ferrer i Guàrdia, 13 • www.poble-espanyol.com • 935 086 300 • €€€ • Metro: Espanya

### CosmoCaixa

**4** This science museum brings planet Earth and outer space into sharper focus for kids and grown-ups. Attractions include the **Planetarium,** offering different shows during the day, and the **Flooded Forest,** a reproduction Amazon rain forest with piranhas, anacondas, and other jungle creatures. The museum holds a range

**Huge aquariums in CosmoCaixa hold underwater creatures from the rain forest.**

of workshops, from **Toca, Toca!,** an activity giving kids a chance to touch creatures, to the interactive **Clik** for older children.

Carrer d'Isaac Newton 26 • www.obrasocial.lacaixa.es • 932 126 050 • € • Closed Mon., Jan. 1, 6, Dec. 25 • Metro: Avinguda Tibidabo

## Tibidabo

**5** Barcelona's amusement park blends the bygone thrills of the Talaia spinning arm (1921) and Avio airplane (1928) with new thrills like the bright-red Muntanya Russa rollercoaster with a 100-foot (30 m) vertical drop and 3.5 g-force. A smaller section of the park caters to younger children.

Plaça del Tibidabo 3-4 • www.tibidabo.cat • 932 117 942 • €€€€€• Check website for opening times • FGC: Av. Tibidabo (Tramvia Blau or 196 bus, then Funicular del Tibidabo)

## Torre de Collserola

**6** Set in a futuristic television tower on Tibidabo mountain, this is the highest observation point over the city.

Carretera de Vallvidrera al Tibidabo • www.torredecollserola.com • 932 117 942 • € • Check website for opening times • Metro: Peu del Funicular

# PART 2

# Barcelona's Neighborhoods

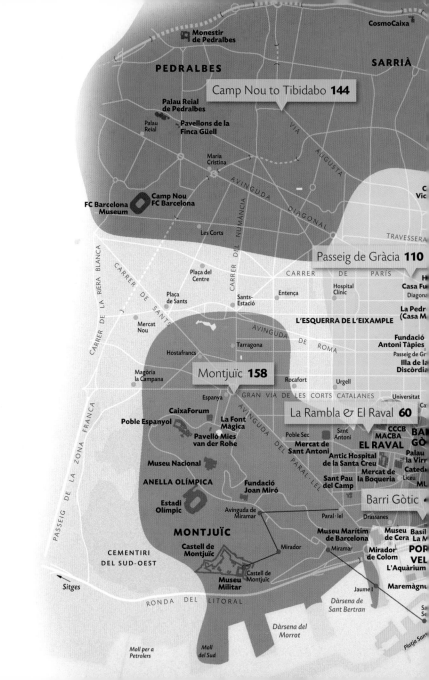

CosmoCaixa

Monestir
de Pedralbes

PEDRALBES

SARRIÀ

Camp Nou to Tibidabo **144**

Palau Reial
de Pedralbes

Palau
Reial

Pavellons de la
Finca Güell

VIA AUGUSTA

Maria
Cristina

AVINGUDA

C
Vic

DIAGONAL

Camp Nou
FC Barcelona

FC Barcelona
Museum

TRAVESSERA

Les Corts

CARRER DEL NUMANCIA

Plaça del
Centre

CARRER DE PARÍS

Passeig de Gràcia **110**

CARRER DE LA RIERA BLANCA

CARRER DE SANTS

Plaça
de Sants

Sants-
Estació

Entença

Hospital
Clínic

Casa Fu
Diagona

La Pedr
(Casa M

Mercat
Nou

Hostafrancs

AVINGUDA

Tarragona

DE ROMA

L'ESQUERRA DE L'EIXAMPLE

Fundació
Antoni Tàpies

Passeig de Gr

Magòria
la Campana

Montjuïc **158**

Rocafort

Urgell

Illa de la
Discòrdia

Universitat

Espanya

GRAN VIA DE LES CORTS CATALANES

Ca

CaixaForum

AVINGUDA DEL PARAL·LEL

La Rambla & El Raval **60**

Poble Espanyol

La Font
Màgica

Pavelló Mies
van der Rohe

Poble Sec

Sant
Antoni

CCCB
MACBA

BA
GÒ

EL RAVAL

Palau
la Virr

PASSEIG DE LA ZONA FRANCA

Museu Nacional

Mercat de
Sant Antoni

Antic Hospital
de la Santa Creu

Cated

ANELLA OLÍMPICA

Fundació
Joan Miró

Sant Pau
del Camp

Mercat de
la Boqueria

Liceu

ML

Estadi
Olímpic

Avinguda de Miramar

Paral·lel

Barri Gòtic

MONTJUÏC

Drassanes

CEMENTIRI
DEL SUD-OEST

Castell de
Montjuïc

Mirador

Museu Marítim
de Barcelona

Museu
de Cera

Basíl
La M

Miramar

Mirador
de Colom

POR
VEL

Museu
Militar

Castell de
Montjuïc

L'Aquàrium

Sitges

Jaume I

Maremàgnu

Sa
Se

RONDA DEL LITORAL

Dàrsena de
Sant Bertran

Dàrsena del
Morrot

Moll per a
Petrolers

Moll
del Sud

Platja San

# Barcelona's Neighborhoods

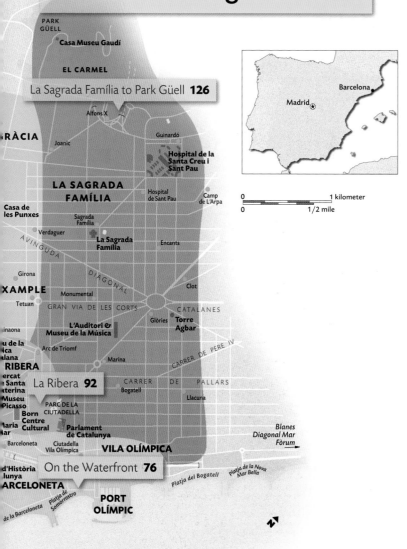

PARK GÜELL

Casa Museu Gaudí

EL CARMEL

La Sagrada Família to Park Güell **126**

Alfons X

RÀCIA

Joanic

Guinardó

Hospital de la
Santa Creu i
Sant Pau

**LA SAGRADA
FAMÍLIA**

Hospital
de Sant Pau

Camp
de L'Arpa

Casa de
les Punxes

Sagrada
Família

Verdaguer

**La Sagrada
Família**

Encants

Girona

AVINGUDA

DIAGONAL

Clot

XAMPLE

Monumental

Tetuan

GRAN VIA DE LES CORTS

CATALANES

inaona

Glòries

**Torre
Agbar**

**L'Auditori &
Museu de la Música**

u de la
ica
alana

Arc de Triomf

Marina

CARRER DE PERE IV

**RIBERA**

ercat
e Santa
aterina

La Ribera **92**

CARRER DE PALLARS

Bogatell

Museu
Picasso

Llacuna

laria
lar

**Born
Centre
Cultural**

PARC DE LA
CIUTADELLA

**Parlament
de Catalunya**

Barceloneta

Ciutadella
Vila Olímpica

**VILA OLÍMPICA**

Blanes
Diagonal Mar
Fòrum

d'Història
lunya

On the Waterfront **76**

ARCELONETA

Platja de la Nova
Mar Bella

Platja del Bogatell

de la Barceloneta

Platja de
Somorrostro

**PORT
OLÍMPIC**

Barcelona

Madrid

0        1 kilometer
0        1/2 mile

*Mediterranean Sea*

# Barri Gòtic

The old town's medieval core lies between La Rambla and the busy Via Laietana, and is bordered to the north by Plaça de Catalunya and to the south by Port Vell. Known as the Gothic Quarter, the area was built on the remains of the early Roman settlement, Barcino. At first the city was confined within the fourth-century Roman walls, but it eventually spread beyond them. Wandering through the narrow lanes of Barri Gòtic, you can sense the history of the city and identify the different eras in the layers of old stone. Discover remnants of the medieval Jewish community that lived here until 1492 when the Jews were expelled from Spain. Today, the area holds many attractions: See the comings and goings of today's seat of government, linger over coffee in a quiet courtyard, or enjoy the cultural vibrancy of the contemporary city in art galleries and fashion boutiques. Above all, take time to explore the small streets and open entranceways to the many old mansions here.

◖ **Visitors on a bike
tour pause to
admire Barcelona's
Gothic cathedral.**

# Barri Gòtic

*Discover the ancient heart of the city amid the historic winding lanes of the Gothic quarter.*

**① Plaça de la Vila de Madrid** (see p. 48) Walk south from the top of La Rambla, turn left onto Canuda into this quiet square. Look at the Roman necropolis before following D'en Bot. Cross busy shopping street Portaferrissa to find Plaça del Pi, off Petritxol.

**② Plaça del Pi** (see pp. 48–49) Emerging into the square, you face Santa Maria del Pi church. The pine tree (*"pi"* in Catalan) lends its name to the church. Cut across the adjacent square and onto Banys Nous.

**⑤ Plaça de Sant Felip Neri** (see p. 50, 58) A boutique hotel, eccentric shoe museum, and school make unlikely neighbors in this square. Exit via Montjuïc del Bisbe, then go left until you reach Plaça Nova and Avinguda de la Catedral.

**⑥ Catedral (La Seu)** (see p. 51) In an opening between the remains of the Roman wall, the city's main cathedral towers above the surrounding buildings. Follow Comtes past the Museu Frederic Marès and turn left after the Palau del Lloctinent.

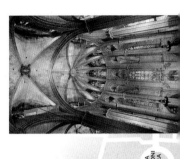

**7 MUHBA Plaça del Rei** (see pp. 54–55) Discover Barcelona's main history museum in this monumental medieval square flanked by a former royal palace. Return to Plaça de Sant Jaume and walk along Llibreteria, then take Ciutat until it becomes Regomir.

**8 Porta del Mar** (see p. 52) The Pati Llimona civic center complex incorporates Porta del Mar. This was the entrance to the Roman city from the sea. Follow Regomir toward the port, turning right onto Ample.

**9 Basílica de la Mercè** (see pp. 52–53) Dedicated to La Mare de Déu de La Mercè, Our Lady of Mercy, city patroness, this church has an emotional meaning for the people of Barcelona. Continue on Ample and turn right on Nou de Sant Francesc until it narrows into Vidre and you emerge in the luminous Plaça Reial.

wonderful display of berets and panamas in Obach's shop window, turn left into the Call. Meander through the tiny streets of the medieval Jewish district. Then walk through the Call to the square at the end.

**4 Plaça de Sant Jaume** (see p. 50) Two major buildings, the Palau de la Generalitat, seat of the Catalan government, and the Casa de la Ciutat, or Town Hall, dominate this handsome square. Take Bisbe and pass under the neo-Gothic bridge, turn left, then right after Hotel Neri.

**10 Plaça Reial** (see p. 53) This majestic 19th-century arcaded square is a perfect place to relax after a long day or to begin a night out.

OEL BISBE

MUHBA
Plaça del Rei

Catedral
(La Seu)

Plaça
de Sant
Jaume

CARRER DE JAUME I

PLAÇA DE SANT JUST

Jaume I

C. DEL SOTS-TINENT NAVARRO

VIA LAIETANA

C. DE B

C. DEL CALL

The Call
3

CARRER DE FERRAN

PLAÇA DEL PI

PLAÇA DE
SANT
MIQUEL

CARRER DE LA CIUTAT

Porta
del Mar
8

C. DEL REGOMIR

C. D'EN
RAURIC

CARRER DE D'AVINYÓ

AMPLE

Basílica de
la Mercè
9

Plaça
Reial
10

CARRER DE COLOM

PASSEIG DE COLOM

C. NOU SANT FRANCESC

Metro:
Drassanes

| 0 | 150 meters |
| 0 | 150 yards |

**BARRI GÒTIC DISTANCE: 1.6 MILES (2.5 KM)**
**TIME: APPROX. 8 HOURS METRO START: CATALUNYA**

### Plaça de la Vila de Madrid

**1** This pleasant residential square has a curious centerpiece—a Roman graveyard, dating from the first to third century A.D. Discovered only in the 1950s, the graveyard would have been outside the Roman city walls. On the corner of Canuda, the 18th-century **Palau Savassona** houses a members-only cultural center, the **Ateneu.** Check the calendar posted inside the grand carriage entrance for a program of events open to the public. Head to the terrace restaurant in the Ateneu to enjoy breakfast in the early morning sun.

Plaça de la Vila de Madrid, off Canuda • Metro: Catalunya

### Plaça del Pi

**2** On your way to the square, you will walk along Petritxol, a street bristling with overhanging balconies, interesting shops, and art galleries including one of the oldest in the city, **Sala Parés.** On entering the square, look for the spectacular window displays of fierce

**The elegant buildings in Plaça del Pi provide a charming backdrop for shopping or strolling.**

implements at the knife shop, **Ganiveteria Roca**, dating from 1911. The fortresslike facade of **Santa Maria del Pi** (see p. 57) dominates the square. Built between 1319 and 1391, the church is pure Catalan Gothic (see pp. 56–57). The beautiful rose window was restored by Jujol, one of Gaudí's close associates, after being damaged in the Spanish Civil War. Visit the crypt and see the church treasures with a tourist ticket (€€). Artists display their work in Plaça del Pi and the adjacent square, **Plaça de Sant Josep Oriol,** on weekends (all-day Saturday and Sunday a.m.). On the first and third weekends of the month, a market sells artisan-made products that include cheeses, honey, chocolate, and bread.

Plaça del Pi & Plaça de Sant Josep Oriol • Metro: Liceu

## The Call

**3** The Jewish quarter, the Call, thrived in the medieval period until anti-Jewish attacks decimated the community in 1391. In 1492, Spain expelled all Jews. Turn onto **Arc de Sant Ramón del Call** and follow a route traced out on metal signs through the main part of the quarter, the Call Major. In **Marlet,** a wall tablet etched in Hebrew pays tribute to a rabbi who founded a hospital for the poor on the site. **MUHBA** (History Museum of Barcelona; *Placeta de Manuel Ribé*) has a small branch here, explaining aspects of Jewish life. The sun barely filters through to the narrow streets where today you will find craft shops, tiny cafés, and candlelit bars. In **La Basilica Galeria** (*Sant Sever, 7*), feast your eyes on the eccentric goods ranging from cockroach necklaces to wooden purses.

Carrer del Call • 932 562 122 • € (see Savvy Traveler box p. 55) • Closed Mon., p.m. Tues.–Fri., and public holidays • Metro: Liceu or Jaume I

### GOOD **EATS**

■ **BUENAS MIGAS**
Specializing in focaccias, the Anglo-Italian owners of this restaurant also offer many homemade dishes that are ideal for lunch. **Baixada de Santa Clara, 2, 933 191 380, €**

■ **CAFÈ DE L'ACADÈMIA**
A reservation is essential at this highly regarded, reasonably priced restaurant. You will find delicious Catalan food with a contemporary twist, in charming Gothic surroundings. **Plaça Sant Just, 933 198 253, closed weekends, €€€**

■ **CAFÈ DE L'ESTIU**
Head to the secluded courtyard of the Museu Frederic Marés, once the garden of the Palau Reial, for snacks and drinks. Listen to the chimes from the cathedral belfry towering above. **Plaça de Sant Iu, 5–6, 933 103 014, closed Oct.–March, €**

**BARRI GÒTIC**

## Plaça de Sant Jaume

**4** After the labyrinthine lanes of the Call, this wide-open square comes as a surprise with its bright sunlight and formal lines. Here you can see and feel the business of government, as people in dark suits and official cars head to the **Palau de la Generalitat** (*Plaça de Sant Jaume, 4, www.gencat.cat, 934 024 600, open April 23, Sept. 11, Sept. 24, or/and 2nd and 4th weekend of each month, advance reservation required*), center of the Catalan government, guarded by the Mossos d'Esquadra, the Catalan police. Across the cobbled square stands the **Casa de la Ciutat** (*Plaça de Sant Jaume, 1, tel 010 (general information, open Sun. 10 a.m.–1:30 p.m., all day Feb. 11, April 23*), home to the Ajuntament, city council, safeguarded by the less showy Guàrdia Urbana, local city police. Appropriately, in Roman times, this was the home of the forum. Both buildings contain Gothic elements behind newer facades (see Catalan Gothic pp. 56–57).

Plaça de Sant Jaume, 4 • Metro: Jaume I

## Plaça de Sant Felip Neri

**5** Stop to listen to the trickling of the fountain as you absorb the historic atmosphere of this tiny square, hidden in the shadows of the cathedral. In 1938, during the Spanish Civil War, a fascist bomb killed 42 people, mostly children; the scars on the pale stone facade of Sant Felip Neri church still testify to this tragedy. The curious **Museu del Calçat** (Shoe Museum) (see p. 142) proudly displays an eclectic collection, from a shoe belonging to Catalan cellist Pau Casals to a giant shoe made-to-measure for a statue of Columbus at the end of La Rambla. Enjoy a prelunch aperitif in the outdoor terrace of boutique **Neri Hotel** (entrance Sant Sever, 5), once a medieval palace.

Plaça de Sant Felip Neri • Metro: Catalunya or Jaume I

## Catedral (La Seu)

**6** Stand back to enjoy the panorama of street artists, tour groups, dogwalkers, and, on weekends, *sardana* dancers (see p. 73) on the large esplanade at the foot of the city's main cathedral. As you walk up the steps past the Roman watchtowers, notice the later additions and see how the different periods of history left their mark. Built on the site of an earlier Romanesque church, the current cathedral dates from 1298. The side chapels, dedicated to various saints, including Rita, saint of the impossible, are elaborately decorated and contain notable altarpieces and paintings by Catalan Gothic artists including Bernat Martorell and Bartolomé Bermejo.

A remnant of the Romanesque structure that became part of the cathedral, the Santa Llúcia chapel was built in 1268, making it the oldest part of the complex. Buy a tourist ticket *(1 p.m.–5 p.m., €€)* to see the ornately carved choir stalls, visit the museum, and take an elevator ride to the roof for a bird's-eye view of the city spires. You may hear the sound of the geese that reside in the cloister pool as you walk through the cathedral. Allow time to stroll around the exterior of the cathedral to see details such as gargoyles, inscribed tablets, and sculptures.

**Visit the cloisters and see the pond where 13 geese seem to be in charge. The number of geese represents the age at which St. Eulàlia, co-patroness of Barcelona, was martyred.**

Plaça de la Seu, 3 • www.catedralbcn.org • 933 151 554 • Metro: Catalunya or Urquinaona

## MUHBA Plaça del Rei

**7** See pp. 54–55.

Plaça del Rei • www.museuhistoria.bcn.cat • 932 562 100 • €€ • Closed Mon., Jan. 1, May 1, June 24, Dec. 25 • Metro: Jaume I, Liceu, or Catalunya

**BARRI GÒTIC**

## Porta del Mar

**8** The main entrance to the ancient Roman city, the Porta del Mar remained hidden behind centuries of new building until the 1980s. Construction work on a civic center, the Patí Llimona, revealed the Porta del Mar, part of a Roman wall, and a medieval palace. Enter the Pati Limona for a closer look at the remains and you may also catch a temporary photography exhibition. Back outside, do not miss the tiny 16th-century chapel dedicated to St. Christopher, protector of travelers. In a long-established tradition, a priest still blesses vehicles on this spot on July 10, which the city celebrates as St. Christopher's feast day. Look through the window of the next building to glimpse the remains of Roman thermal baths. In the first century B.C., the sea extended inland, near the baths, and may have filled them with salt water. You can see the baths on a guided tour (advance reservation required).

Regomir, 3 and Regomir, 7–9 • 932 562 122 • www.museuhistoria.bcn.cat • €
• Metro: Jaume I or Liceu

## Basílica de la Mercè

**9** The ornate baroque architecture of La Mercè, built in 1765, contrasts with the austere Catalan Gothic cathedral and the Roman sites. The warm shades of marble and the heavily gilded altars are almost oppressive, but it remains a much-loved church, dedicated to Our Lady of Mercy, the co-patroness of Barcelona. During the La Mercè fiesta, the main festival celebrating Our Lady, local dignitaries come to Mass here accompanied by *gegants, castellers,* and all the festive accoutrements (see pp. 72–73). Even the Barcelona soccer team sometimes visits the church to give thanks after a particularly important victory. The dome, adorned by a statue of the Virgin precariously holding her child, forms a striking part of the city skyline when seen from the port. Dense housing in front of

### SAVVY **TRAVELER**

Plan your visit to coincide with one of Barcelona's main fiestas, such as La Mercè. For several days around September 24, the city celebrates its patroness, Our Lady of Mercy. Celebrations around February 12 honor her co-patroness, Santa Eulàlia.

**The elaborate, gilded baroque interior of the Basilica de la Mercè features intricate stucco.**

the church was demolished in the 1980s to make a square, one of the first urban spaces to be created in the city's regeneration program.

Plaça de la Mercè, 1 • 933 190 190 • Metro: Drassanes

## Plaça Reial

**10** Francesc Daniel Molina built this handsome neoclassical square on the site of a convent in 1848. Antoni Gaudí, at the age of 27, designed two of its lampposts in 1879. On Sunday mornings, amid the trendy surroundings of the square, an outdoor market sells stamps and coins, an authentic reminder of an older Barcelona. As well as an eclectic mix of bars, restaurants, and clubs (see p. 74), the square hosts live concerts at fiesta time.

Plaça Reial • Metro: Liceu or Drassanes

# MUHBA Plaça del Rei

*The very walls and foundations of this museum are historic: Below the medieval palace lie Roman ruins. Explore both to discover the city's history.*

These pits were once used to dye and clean Roman cloth.

The Plaça del Rei, built on Roman ruins, was once the royal palace of the counts of Barcelona and rulers of the Crown of Aragón, who held court in the ancient palace halls. Today, the complex is home to MUHBA, History Museum of Barcelona. Begin your visit beneath the medieval foundations where you can see the 2,000-year-old remains of the Roman city. Then return to ground level where exhibits in the medieval palace buildings, the Saló del Tinell and the Capella de Santa Àgata, reveal the city's evolution.

### Casa Padellàs

Begin your visit in a medieval mansion, now housing the museum entrance and bookshop. The Casa Padellàs was moved here from a nearby street, stone by stone. Start the audio-guided tour as you pass a display of Roman statues and artifacts of daily life. Then watch an audiovisual presentation showing how the city developed over the centuries.

### Archaeological Site

Take an elevator down beneath the medieval palace to the Roman foundation, where the daily routine of a Roman city comes to life amid small villas and workshops. Raised walkways lead over the preserved ruins of the Roman colony: Colonia Iulia Augusta Paterna Faventia Barcino. Information boards explain how sentinels guarded the city from watchtowers. Discover the manufacturing stages of a Roman delicacy, *garum,* made from salted preserved fish. Highlights are: the *fullonica* and *tinctoria,* where clothes were laundered and dyed, a wine workshop, and a stone game revealing a rare glimpse of a Roman child's life.

### Saló del Tinell

Continue the tour in the Royal Palace, where the scale of the rooms reflects the influence of the medieval counts of Barcelona. They ruled Aragón from the somber Saló del Tinell, where wide vaulting creates a spacious feel.

### Capella de Santa Àgata

The delicate 14th-century **Chapel of St. Agatha** contrasts with the bold lines of the Tinell. Light streams through the high, stained-glass windows. Leave the chapel and pause on the rounded steps that lead out of the building down to Plaça del Rei. According to legend, the monarchs Ferdinand and Isabella received Columbus here on his return from the New World.

Plaça del Rei • www.museuhistoria.bcn.cat • 932 562 100 • €€ • Closed Mon., Jan. 1, May 1, June 24, Dec. 25 • Metro: Jaume I, Liceu, or Catalunya

**BARRI GÒTIC**

# Catalan Gothic

Barcelona takes its main architectural identity from the Gothic movement, which began in France in the early 13th century and lasted until the Renaissance. Enriched by Catalonia's expansion, the wealthy merchant class paid for many new buildings adapted from the Gothic style. Simple, sturdy, and well portioned with few frills, Catalan Gothic absorbed northern influences and took on a distinctive look that gave the oldest part of the city its name.

**The medieval buildings of the Palau Reial (above) contain Catalan Gothic gems such as the Saló del Tinell and Casa Padellàs. The tympanum over the entrance to Santa Maria del Mar (right) features a widened Catalan Gothic arch, with a sculpture of Christ flanked by the Virgin and St. John.**

Gothic architecture developed with the territorial expansion and mercantile wealth that saw the flowering of Catalan culture, with troubadors and poets, painters and builders enhancing the city.

### Distinctive Elements

The defining characteristic of Gothic architecture is the pointed arch, which replaced the Romanesque round arch. But in Barcelona a further refinement created a wider arch, especially on doorways.

Another major feature of northern Gothic was the introduction of flying buttresses, exterior structural stone pillars that held up the side walls of churches to allow the building to climb closer to heaven. Barcelona's builders gave more emphasis to breadth than height to create a better-proportioned interior. This lack of elevation reduced the space for windows in the upper part of the building; instead, a large rose window often decorated the west facade, such as the one in **Santa Maria del Pi** (see pp. 49, 57). Roofs did not rise high—some are even flat—and they have few pinnacles and spires.

Pillars and towers, round in most Gothic architecture, evolved to include the angular lines of hexagons and octagons as in the pillars in the nave in **Santa Maria del Mar,** regarded as the purest and best proportioned Catalan Gothic church.

## Civic Buildings

In secular buildings the style reached a high point in the huge vaulted **Saló del Tinell** (see p. 55), the royal great hall. Catalan Gothic spread to important civic buildings, including the town hall and stock exchange (La Llotja). Rich merchants paid for this work and built their own mansions with modest facades, courtyards, balconies, and distinctive windows that can still be seen, notably on **Carrer de Montcada.**

## GOTHIC **CHURCHES**

**Basílica dels Sants Màrtirs Just i Pastor**
A single nave and polygonal apse form a simple space; see sculptures of the martyrs over the portal. **Plaça de Sant Just, 6, www .basilicasantjust.cat**

**Santa Anna** Tucked away in a small square, Santa Anna, founded by the Knights Templar, has a tranquil two-story cloister. **Santa Anna, 29**

**Santa Maria del Pi**
This church features rare medieval stained glass and holds recitals in the crypt. **Plaça del Pi, www .basilicadelpi.com**

# Squares & Outdoor Spaces

People gather to chat, sell their wares, dance, or demonstrate in open areas known as *plaça* in Catalan (*plaza* in Spanish). In common with many European cities, Barcelona has a range of squares, from large spaces overlooked by tall buildings, to small gaps in the urban sprawl with a shady bench to take a break.

■ PLAÇA DE SANT FELIP NERI

Explore the winding lanes in the Gothic quarter to find this atmospheric square (see p. 50). Enjoy the heady aromas wafting from a handmade soap shop as you explore the historic sites. Admire the baroque **Sant Felip Neri** church, discover a shoe museum, and look out for the café used in Woody Allen's film *Vicky Cristina Barcelona*.

Metro: Liceu or Jaume I

■ PLAÇA SANT JUST

In a corner of this Barri Gòtic square you will find one of the oldest churches in

Cars are banned in Plaça Sant Felip Neri, so explore on foot or by bicycle.

Barcelona, **Basílica dels Sant Màrtirs Just i Pastor** (see p. 57). St. Just appears on the square's Gothic fountain, which brought running water to the area as early as 1427. In the summer, local eateries set up tables outside for alfresco dining. In early November, the locals celebrate All Saints' Day by serving roast chestnuts and sweet muscatel wine at a *castanyada* (chestnut) party. A traditional family-run grocery continues to trade from the ground floor of the **Palau Moxó,** an 18th-century palace.

Metro: Jaume I

### ■ ARC DE TRIOMF & PASSEIG LLUÍS COMPANYS

In La Ribera, the Arc de Triomf and the broad avenue leading to **Parc de la Ciutadella** (see pp. 34, 100–101) create a spacious venue for events. *Modernista* architect, Josep Vilaseca i Casanovas, designed the redbrick arch in the neo-Mudéjar style as the main entrance to the 1888 Universal Exhibition. Walk from the arch, along the avenue, and look for the monumental **Palau de Justícia,** the law courts. Notice the lampposts designed by Pere Falqués, who also made the benches with lamps on **Passeig de Gràcia.** On weekends the area fills with dog-walkers and cyclists.

Metro: Arc de Triomf

### ■ LA TORRE DE LES AIGÜES

All over Eixample, blocks are designed around a large inner patio. In the 1980s, La Torre de les Aigües became the first block to open its courtyard to the public (see p. 141). Also known as the "Eixample beach," this patio has a shallow pool, where toddlers splash in summer. Admire the sturdy 19th-century water tower as you enjoy the inside view of a typical Eixample block.

Roger de Llúria, 56 • Pool open late June–early Sept. • Metro: Passeig de Gràcia or Girona

### ■ PARC DE JOAN MIRÓ

Near the base of Montjuïc, Parc de Joan Miró (see p. 141) became the first new urban space in Barcelona in 1983. The park contains pines and palms, bougainvilleas and oleanders, play areas, and a library. Built on the site of a former slaughterhouse, the park also has another name, Parc de l'Escorxador ("slaughterhouse"). The area occupies the equivalent of four city blocks, arranged on different levels. Do not miss the colorful, tiled 70-foot (21 m) Joan Miró sculpture, **"Dona i Ocell"** ("Woman and Bird").

Metro: Espanya or Tarragona.

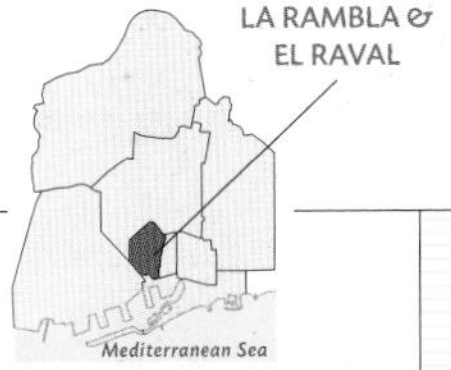


# La Rambla & El Raval

A stroll down La Rambla offers a 24-hour spectacle: Amble past flower sellers and human statues by day, and elegant operagoers and rowdy revelers by night. The colorful avenue of La Rambla runs for 0.75 mile (1.2 km) from Plaça de Catalunya to the waterfront, separating the El Raval district from the Gothic quarter. Dip into the narrow streets of El Raval to discover an area undergoing a transformation. Once known for convents and churches, the neighborhood became notorious in the 20th century for brothels and overcrowded housing. Recent regeneration programs have swept through the area, bringing new university departments, cultural centers, and trendy boutiques. A melting pot of families and bohemians now live side by side in this ever changing district.



**◀ Colorful flower stalls are one of the many attractions that draw visitors to La Rambla.**

# La Rambla & El Raval

*Stroll along the vibrant, colorful Rambla and dip into the side streets of El Raval in the heart of the old city.*

**2 Museu d'Art Contemporani de Barcelona (MACBA)** (see p. 64) The Plaça dels Àngels is dominated by Richard Meier's MACBA, the dazzling white Contemporary Art Museum that opened in 1995. Turn left from the museum onto Montalegre to reach the CCCB.

**3 Centre de Cultura Contemporània de Barcelona (CCCB)** (see p. 65) This former hospice has been converted into a dynamic center for exhibitions and events on contemporary urban issues. Wander through the rear courtyard, past MACBA, and take Àngels as far as Carme.

**4 Antic Hospital de la Santa Creu** (see p. 66) An arched entrance leads into this atmospheric medieval hospital and garden complex, now home to various civic bodies. Return to La Rambla along Carme.

**5 Palau de la Virreina** (see p. 66) Find out what's on in town from the information center in this palace. Farther along La Rambla is La Boqueria.

**1 Font de les Canaletes** (see p. 64) A landmark near the top of La Rambla, this drinking fountain is a favorite meeting place. Turn right at the *modernista* pharmacy, Nadal, and head for the 16th-century Convent dels Àngels at the end of Elisabets.

Universitat

CARRER DE PELAI

CARRER DELS TALLERS

PLAÇA DE CASTELLA

CARRER DE VALLDONZELLA

C DE MONTALEGRE

PLAÇA DELS ÀNGELS

Catalunya

Font de les Canaletes

LA RAMBLA

Centre de Cultura Contemporània de Barcelona (CCCB) **3**

Museu d'Art Contemporani de Barcelona (MACBA) **2**

C DEL S ÀNGELS

C DE J. COSTA

CARRER DE LA RIERA ALTA

p. 69) Amble up this wide avenue, created to regenerate the area. Enjoy the street art and alfresco dining.

**9 Sant Pau del Camp** (see p. 68)
Deep in the heart of today's multicultural Raval, the church remains a place of calm surrounded by late-night supermarkets and trendy bars. Retrace your steps to find the open space and palm trees of the new Rambla.

**6 Mercat de la Boqueria**
(see p. 67) The city's largest market has plenty of places to eat, so stop for a snack. Continue down La Rambla through the flower stalls.

**7 Gran Teatre del Liceu** (see p. 68)
When you reach the Joan Miró pavement mosaic, look up to see the elegant entrance to the venerated opera house. Continue past the Hotel Husa Oriente and turn right on Nou de la Rambla.

**8 Palau Güell** (see pp. 70–71) The town house Gaudí designed in 1885 looms up amid storefronts and ordinary apartment buildings. Return to La Rambla and turn left after the Liceu, following Sant Pau to the end.

200 meters
200 yards

**LA RAMBLA & EL RAVAL  DISTANCE: 1.6 MILES (2.5 KM)**
**TIME: APPROX. 8 HOURS  METRO START: CATALUNYA**

## SAVVY **TRAVELER**

Pickpockets are a less attractive aspect of La Rambla's fame. The streetwise can avoid this danger by staying alert and keeping valuables close. Be wary of groups known as *traileros,* who encourage tourists to gamble in a game similar to the three-card trick. The "bystanders," often accomplices, make it look easy. But don't be duped—you'll never win.

## Font de les Canaletes

1 The first stretch of La Rambla is named Rambla de Canaletes, after an ornate 19th-century drinking fountain. A plaque explains the tradition that once you have tasted its waters you are sure to return to Barcelona. This popular meeting place explodes with life when the beloved local Barça soccer team wins an important match. Jubilant fans descend from all parts of the city, chanting and setting off flares around the fountain. Look down under the main spouts to see an additional, low-lying spout for thirsty dogs.

Rambla de Canaletes • Metro: Catalunya

## Museu d'Art Contemporani de Barcelona (MACBA)

2 Along with the adjoining Centre de Cultura Contemporània de Barcelona (CCCB), the Contemporary Art Museum was part of a major urban and cultural regeneration policy begun by farsighted local authorities in the 1980s. The collection covers artists from the postwar years to the present day, notably Catalan artists such as the Dau al Set group founded by visual poet Joan Brossa in Barcelona in 1948, plus Spanish and international artists. A full calendar includes avant-garde temporary exhibitions and talks. The whiter than white building, characteristic of the American architect Richard Meier, may be more of an attraction than the art, while the square in front of the museum has grown into a community space, forming a perfect venue for skateboarders, impromptu soccer matches, and concerts. Check the MACBA calendar for late-night openings, especially the Nits d'Estiu ("summer nights"), when the museum bar offers drinks and tapas into the night.

Plaça dels Àngels, 1 • www.macba.cat • 934 120 810 • €€ • Closed Tues., Jan. 1, Dec. 25 • Metro: Catalunya or Universitat

### Centre de Cultura Contemporània de Barcelona (CCCB)

**3** Discover something new in the stimulating program of exhibitions, dance performances, seminars, festivals, films, and lectures, all dealing with contemporary urban issues, put on by the Center for Contemporary Culture. The building itself inspires awe; once an abandoned Casa de la Caritat (poorhouse), the old structure and courtyard have been transformed into a 21st-century cultural center, which contains auditoriums and exhibition space. Combining original features with striking innovations, such as the glass wall in the courtyard that has an escalator taking you to a lookout point, this complex demonstrates Barcelona's inimitable habit of fusing old and new. The cultural center's C3Bar (see p. 124) has a terrace opening onto a square behind the CCCB. On the other sides of the square are MACBA and Ramon Llull University.

Montalegre, 5 • www.cccb.org • 933 064 100 • € • Closed Mon., Jan. 1, Dec. 24–25 and 31 • Metro: Catalunya or Universitat

LA RAMBLA & EL RAVAL

Centers like MACBA have brought new life to El Raval and created open spaces for dining.

## GOOD **EATS**

■ **CAFÉ DE L'OPERA**
Sip coffee or enjoy an aperitif in the early evening with the operagoing crowd. Large mirrors and marble top tables give this café a fin de siècle atmosphere. **La Rambla, 74**, 933 177 585, €

■ **CASA LEOPOLDO**
Enjoy fine fish amid the tiled walls of this traditional restaurant, run by three generations of the same family for more than 80 years. **Sant Rafael, 24**, 934 413 014, €€€€

■ **KASPARO**
This popular outdoor café under the arches in a quiet square near La Rambla serves sandwiches with an imaginative range of fillings, salads, and a creative dish of the day. **Plaça Vicenç Martorell, 4,** 933 022 072, €€

## Antic Hospital de la Santa Creu

The construction of this medieval hospital complex began in 1401, and it remained in use for centuries. In 1926, Gaudí died here, after he had been run over by a tram (see p. 137). The buildings are now home to the **Massana School** (an art institute), the **Biblioteca Nacional de Catalunya** (national library), and other institutions. The former convalescent center on the right of the Carme street entrance now houses the **Institut d'Estudis Catalans** (Institute for Catalan Studies). It is usually closed to the public, so peer in to admire the glazed decorative tiles and porticoed courtyard. Opposite stands the **Reial Acadèmia de Medicina** (an academic medical institute), where every Wednesday morning, you may visit the surprisingly sumptuous anatomy room. Jacaranda blossoms fill the peaceful cloistered garden in May, making spring an ideal time to visit.

Carme, 47 or Hospital, 56 • Closed Sun. • Metro: Catalunya or Liceu

## Palau de la Virreina

Spain's Viceroy to Peru commissioned this baroque palace for his return to Barcelona in the late 18th century, but he died shortly after it was completed, so his wife lived here alone and the palace was duly renamed, Virreina ("vicereine"), in her honor. Posters often cover the elegant facade of the palace, advertising the temporary exhibitions on photography and related disciplines, held in the noble rooms within. As the headquarters of the **City Council Cultural Institute,** the information center has everything you need to know about what's happening in Barcelona.

La Rambla, 99 • www.lavirreina.bcn.cat • 933 161 000 • Closed Mon., Jan. 1, May 1, Dec. 25–26 • Metro: Liceu

LA RAMBLA & EL RAVAL

## Mercat de la Boqueria

**6** The largest and most spectacular of Barcelona's 39 food markets has become an essential stop for foodies (see p. 30). Traders have sold food here for centuries, but the current building was constructed on the site of a convent, hence its official name: Mercat de Sant Josep. Stalls are heaped with seasonal vegetables, fruit, wild mushrooms, and nuts. In the central circular area, the daily catch from the Mediterranean and beyond is piled onto mounds of ice. The meat stalls are dramatic, with every part of the carcass on show. Bars sell fresh snacks, making this a good place for a break in the day.

(see p. 30)

La Rambla, 91 • www.boqueria.info • 933 182 584 • Closed Sun. and public holidays • Metro: Liceu

### SAVVY **TRAVELER**

Although the market is open on Mondays, visit from Tuesday to Saturday mornings, when food displays are at their best, or perch on a stool at lunchtime for the freshest grilled fish in town.

**LA RAMBLA & EL RAVAL**

Shrimp is sold fresh or cooked, and in a range of sizes, at La Boqueria.

### Gran Teatre del Liceu

**7** Founded in 1847, this elegant opera house has had a turbulent history, surviving two fires and, in 1893, an anarchist bomb that killed 20 people. After a devastating fire in 1994, local luminaries joined forces to resurrect this popular phoenix from the ashes. By 1999, the restored Liceu reopened, immaculately loyal to the original classical design, but with state-of-the-art technology befitting a leading opera house. Modern features include: Curtains designed by Catalan fashion designer Toni Miró and ceiling paintings by Catalan artist Perejaume. As an 11-year-old, Josep Carreras made his debut here, and soprano Montserrat Caballé celebrated 50 years since her first performance at the Liceu. Recent productions include avant-garde opera and a high-profile ballet season.

La Rambla, 51–59 • www.liceubarcelona.cat • 934 859 900 • Tours €€€
• Metro: Liceu

### Palau Güell

**8** See pp. 70–71.

Nou de la Rambla, 3–5 • www.palauguell.cat • 934 725 775 • €€€ • Closed Mon., Jan. 1 and 6–13, Dec. 25–26 • Metro: Liceu or Drassanes

### Sant Pau del Camp

**9** The name of this church means "Saint Paul of the countryside," or "in the fields," because it was once in a rural setting. Today, this medieval church retains a peaceful atmosphere amid the commercial bustle that has evolved around it. One of the oldest churches in the city, the site contains the tombstone of a tenth-century count of Barcelona. The church and cloisters are all that remain of a large Benedictine monastery, and they are fine examples of Romanesque architecture more commonly seen in rural Catalonia. The simple lines, naïve sculptures, and the fact the church lies off the beaten tourist path make this site particularly charming.

Sant Pau, 101 • 934 410 001 • Metro: Paral·lel

## Rambla del Raval

**10** Not to be confused with the world-famous Rambla, this avenue opened only in 2000. It has a distinctive character, influenced by a mix of cultures and the efforts of local organizations to breathe new life into this hitherto neglected area. Two streets of overcrowded housing were bulldozed to make this palm-tree-lined avenue, which has brought daylight and outsiders into the neighborhood. A luxury 11-story hotel offers cocktails with a view from the rooftop bar. Nearby, the last vestiges of prostitution in the area are holding out in the shadows of the recently opened Filmoteca, the Catalan film theater. At one end of the Rambla, teenagers clamber onto an enormous sculpture of a cat, the unmistakable work of Colombian artist Botero. On weekends, a market sells funky clothes and accessories. A Moroccan stall with *babouches* (exotic slippers) also serves mint tea. Go no farther for dinner: There is a huge choice, from kebabs to gourmet cuisine.

Between Sant Pau and Hospital • Metro: Liceu or Paral·lel

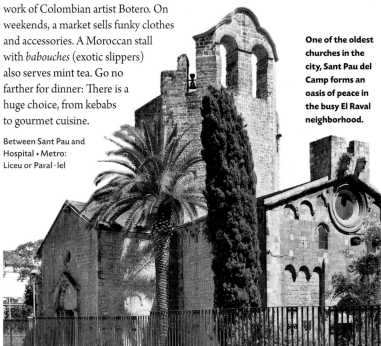

**One of the oldest churches in the city, Sant Pau del Camp forms an oasis of peace in the busy El Raval neighborhood.**

# Palau Güell

*This Gaudí masterpeice, built between 1885 and 1890, displays his signature style in every detail from the basement to the rooftop.*

**The Güell family held parties in the central salon, open to the arched top of the building.**

Wealthy industrialist Eusebi Güell lived in the home the young Antoni Gaudí created for him from 1890 until 1910. Palau Güell includes many of the unique features that characterize Gaudí's work. Take a guided tour through the house to see how Gaudí balanced wildly creative ideas with pragmatic solutions. Start in the stables, where a double staircase and ramp form a passageway for horses, carriages, and people. Then explore the family's rooms, lined with decorative paneling often concealing modern heating and vents.

LA RAMBLA & EL RAVAL

### ■ ENTRANCE & STABLES

Gaudí designed a house that would be discreet from the outside, in an unfashionable neighborhood. Notice the austere facade of stone and heavy wrought iron concealing the opulent bourgeois home within. From outside no one can peer into the building, but Gaudí's ingenious twisted ironwork, means occupants can see out. Begin your tour in the entrance where Gaudí muffled the sound of horses' hooves by making the cobbles from wood. At a time of horse-drawn carriages, Gaudí designed a spiral ramp to a basement stable. Walk down the stairs to see the beautiful brickwork columns. Then go back upstairs to see the more intricate wood carvings and sculpted marble on the residential floors above.

### ■ LIVING AREA & BEDROOMS

The main living area consists of a series of rooms—visitors' reception, smoking room, billiard room, dining room. Follow the tour to visit the rooms, arranged around a central space extending up to the full height of the building. Studded with small skylights,

## IN **THE KNOW**

Palau Güell and Park Güell (see pp. 131–133) are named after Eusebi Güell, who became one of Gaudí's first patrons. Güell had been so impressed by Gaudí's work in the 1878 Paris Expo that he asked him to build a family home: Palau Güell. The two men formed a close working bond across many projects in Barcelona. Güell gave Gaudí the artistic freedom to experiment and evolve a distinctive architectural style.

the cupola overhead floods the house with light from above and from the stained-glass windows. Look out of the bedroom windows on the second level to see into the central hall.

### ■ ATTIC & ROOF TERRACE

Ascend the staircase to the attic, where servants laundered, cooked, and slept. Emerge on the spectacular roof terrace for a panoramic view of the city. Rising out of the curving rooftop, in characteristic Gaudí style, 20 functioning chimneys are beautifully decorated with *trencadís* ceramic mosaics. Each one forms a unique sculpture, and in the center of the roof, the hall spire extends up in a dome.

Nou de la Rambla, 3–5 • www.palauguell.cat • 934 725 775 • €€€ • Closed Mon., Jan. 1 and 6–13, Dec. 25–26 • Metro: Liceu or Drassanes

# Catalan Culture

Catalan culture expresses the distinctive nationality of four provinces—Girona, Lleida, Tarragona, and Barcelona. The Catalan capital is Barcelona, where posters declare, "Catalonia is not Spain." Catalans are proud to be different; they have their own language, flag, and deeply held traditions and festivals. After nearly 40 years of repression by Franco, who banned regional cultures, there has been a Catalan renaissance since the dictator's death in 1975.

Do not miss *castells* (above), displays of human tower building. Teams of *castellers* (the participants) form a strong base, and up to nine stories of people stand on each others' shoulders, topped by a child, the *enxaneta*. Giants (opposite) parade through the city during La Mercè.

### Seny i Rauxa

The Catalan character is said to be marked by two distinctive traits—*seny* (good sense, wisdom) and *rauxa* (creative, passionate recklessness). These traits worked together to produce unique Catalan ideas, such as *modernista* architecture. Gaudí and his contemporaries combined their experimental creativity with a practical understanding of modern life to produce buildings that were artistically novel, yet equipped with heating and ventilation systems.

### Celebrations

The same exuberant spirit sets alight the annual fiestas held in every district. The Catalans have a strong work ethic, but when it's time to party, they celebrate on a grand scale. Barcelona's main fiesta, La Mercè, lasts for nearly a week in September. Giant kings, queens, and fishwives (*gegants*), made of papier-mâché, parade the streets with smaller figures topped by big heads (*capgrossos*). They dance in Plaça de Sant Jaume (see p. 50) in the Gothic quarter, where they mingle with mythical beasts. Human statues are built to dizzying heights, bands play in medieval squares until the small hours, and the city hardly sleeps, but the climax is the Correfoc. Meaning "fire-run," the Correfoc begins when fire-breathing dragons, devils spinning firecrackers, and deafening drummers take over the streets. Things really heat up when people run into the middle of the noisy, fiery scene and dance to taunt the dragons. The Correfoc is definitely not for the fainthearted. Revelers are advised to come prepared for the sparks by wearing protective clothing and glasses.

LA RAMBLA & EL RAVAL

## Sant Jordi

Catalonia's patron saint, Sant Jordi (St. George), is celebrated on April 23 with great seriousness and emotion. In a symbolic gesture to the blood spilled by the slain dragon, men give a red rose to their beloved. In return, the men receive a book, because it is also the day Shakespeare and Cervantes died. La Rambla (see pp. 60–69), lined with bookstalls and rose sellers, becomes packed with proud Catalans enjoying their national day to the full.

## La Sardana

Symbolizing unity, *la sardana* is the solemn national dance, seen at fiestas throughout Catalonia and every weekend in the cathedral square (see p. 51) in Barcelona. Dancers of all ages form large circles by stretching out their arms and holding hands. The delicate, complicated steps are difficult to perform but beautiful to watch.

# Nightlife

Barcelona's nightlife attracts visitors from around the world, and El Raval has a dense concentration of venues in its narrow streets. Most restaurants are open until the early hours as dinner starts late, so there's time to explore. Choose from authentic bodegas to slick clubs, and from exclusive restaurants to beach bars.

**LA RAMBLA & EL RAVAL**

### ■ BOADAS

On the corner of La Rambla and Tallers, this tiny cocktail bar is a Barcelona legend. Opened in the 1930s by Miquel Boadas, who learned his trade in Cuba, its high stools and wooden paneling lined with prints remain unchanged. Don't miss the mojitos.

Tallers, 1 • 933 189 592 • Closed Sun.
• Metro: Catalunya

### ■ PLAÇA REIAL

This majestic square in the Barri Gòtic buzzes from early evening until dawn. To start the evening, enjoy a beer in the bar **Glaciar** *(No. 3, 933 021 163)* or a cocktail in boutique hotel **DO: Plaça Reial** *(No. 1, 934 813 666)*. Later on listen to jazz in **Jamboree** *(No. 17, 933 191 789)* or drink *la última copa* (last drink of the evening) in **Ocaña** *(No. 13–15, 936 764 814)*, the latest cool spot.

### ■ XIRINGUITOS

The waterfront from Barceloneta to Diagonal Mar is lined with lively beach bars, called *xiringuitos*. Many are so popular that they stay open year-round. Bars in the shadow of the **W** hotel or the **Vila Olímpica** (see pp. 84–85) may be more chic, but in between you will find plenty of funky ones. DJs start spinning discs as the sun goes down.

### ■ HOTEL CASA FUSTER

Go to the top of Passeig de Gràcia to see how the other half live. Discover the magic of Barcelona rooftops on summer nights by visiting this luxury five-star hotel's roof bar. The hotel occupies what was once the most opulent private house in the city, designed by *modernista* architect Domènech i Montaner.

Passeig de Gràcia, 132 • 932 553 000
• Metro: Diagonal

**Lights designed by Antoni Gaudí light up the Plaça Reial.**

### ■ SALA RAZZMATAZZ

Near La Sagrada Família, on the borders of the high-tech business district of Poble Nou, discover one of the city's best clubs. With five spaces featuring DJs and regular concerts from national and international bands, the club offers something different each night.

Pamplona, 88 • 933 208 200 • Closed Sun.– Tues. • Metro: Marina or Bogatell

### ■ MONTJUÏC FONT MÀGICA

An old family favorite, the son et lumière shows of the **Font Màgica** against the backdrop of the Palau Nacional never fail to charm the crowds. The illuminated fountains shoot up and down in tune with popular songs.

Plaça Carles Buïgas • Summer: Thurs.–Sun. 9 p.m.–11:30 p.m.; Winter: Thurs.–Fri. 7 p.m.– 9 p.m. • Metro: Espanya

### ■ POBLE ESPANYOL

A little farther up Montjuïc is **Poble Espanyol,** a model Spanish village with restaurants and bars. **El Tablao de Carmen** *(933 256 895)* brings a flavor of Andalucía to Barcelona, with dinner and an authentic flamenco show. Or dance under the stars until dawn in the outdoor club **La Terrazza** *(932 724 980),* which is open until early morning in summer.

Mediterranean Sea

# On the Waterfront

Immerse yourself in the maritime past of this Mediterranean port and enjoy all that it has to offer by following a route around the harbor, across the water, and along the beaches. Recently voted the best beach city in the world, Barcelona's 3 miles (4.8 km) of sandy seafront only emerged after an industrial area was cleared for the 1992 Summer Olympics. Railway lines were rerouted and quayside buildings demolished, which opened up the seafront and port, turning the area into an integral part of the city. Now, tourists and locals alike flock to enjoy the fresh air and Mediterranean Sea, an ever present influence on the city's way of life and culture. As well as boat rides and beaches, the waterfront offers many year-round attractions, from a popular aquarium to sophisticated restaurants and bars.

❶ Barcelona's waterfront has been transformed with wide walkways, encouraging visitors to linger by the sea.

# On the Waterfront

*Take a boat ride around the port, hop a cable car from the harbor, or ride to the top of Columbus's column for the best views of the city.*

**2** **L'Aquàrium** (see p. 81) The second-most visited site in the city after La Sagrada Família. Following your tour, have a coffee on the quayside near the boats, then walk through the shopping mall to Rambla de Mar.

**1** **Museu d'Història de Catalunya** (see pp. 80–81) Housed in a former warehouse, this museum brings Catalan history to life. Head toward the yachts moored in the harbor and turn right. Follow the waterfront and take the landscaped walkway up to the Maremagnum center.

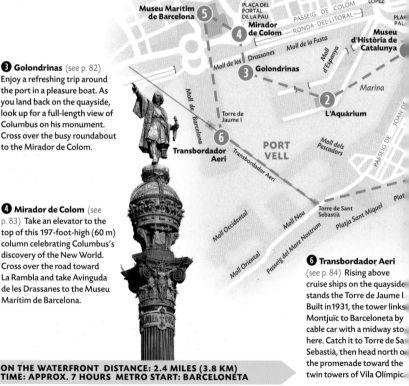

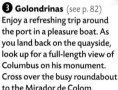

**3** **Golondrinas** (see p. 82) Enjoy a refreshing trip around the port in a pleasure boat. As you land back on the quayside, look up for a full-length view of Columbus on his monument. Cross over the busy roundabout to the Mirador de Colom.

**4** **Mirador de Colom** (see p. 83) Take an elevator to the top of this 197-foot-high (60 m) column celebrating Columbus's discovery of the New World. Cross over the road toward La Rambla and take Avinguda de les Drassanes to the Museu Marítim de Barcelona.

**6** **Transbordador Aeri** (see p. 84) Rising above cruise ships on the quayside stands the Torre de Jaume I. Built in 1931, the tower links Montjuïc to Barceloneta by cable car with a midway stop here. Catch it to Torre de Sant Sebastià, then head north on the promenade toward the twin towers of Vila Olímpica.

**ON THE WATERFRONT  DISTANCE: 2.4 MILES (3.8 KM)
TIME: APPROX. 7 HOURS  METRO START: BARCELONETA**

**❺ Museu Marítim de Barcelona** (see pp. 86–87) Catalonia's long maritime history comes to life in the magnificent setting of the ancient shipyards. The museum's garden offers a shady spot for a cool drink. Cross over Passeig de Josep Carner and skirt the monumental Aduana (Customs) building to the Moll de Barcelona.

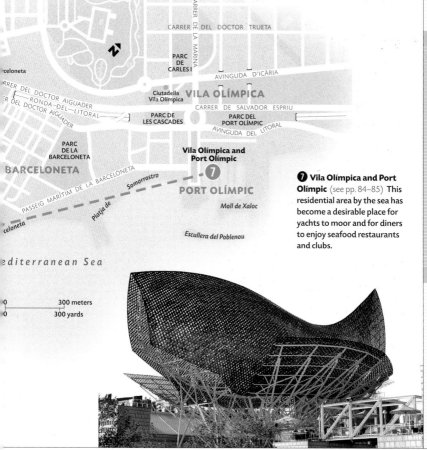

CARRER DE LA MARINA

CARRER DEL DOCTOR TRUETA

PARC DE CARLES I

AVINGUDA D'ICÀRIA

rceloneta

RRER DEL DOCTOR AIGUADER
RONDA DEL LITORAL
ER DEL DOCTOR AIGUADER

Ciutadella Vila Olímpica

**VILA OLÍMPICA**

CARRER DE SALVADOR ESPRIU

PARC DE LES CASCADES

PARC DEL PORT OLÍMPIC

AVINGUDA DEL LITORAL

PARC DE LA BARCELONETA

**BARCELONETA**

PASSEIG MARÍTIM DE LA BARCELONETA

Somorrostro

Platja de

celoneta

**Vila Olímpica and Port Olímpic**

**❼**

**PORT OLÍMPIC**

Moll de Xaloc

Escullera del Poblenou

*editerranean Sea*

| 0 | 300 meters |
| 0 | 300 yards |

**❼ Vila Olímpica and Port Olímpic** (see pp. 84–85) This residential area by the sea has become a desirable place for yachts to moor and for diners to enjoy seafood restaurants and clubs.

## Museu de'Història de Catalunya

**1** The Catalan History Museum takes prime position in the imposing redbrick **Palau de Mar.** The only building to remain from Barcelona's former industrial port, the Palau's cavernous warehouse space provides a spectacular setting for the museum. Ride the long escalators up to the second floor and follow the museum route. Exhibits are arranged chronologically, extending from the Paleolithic period to the dramatic events of 1714, when Spanish troops seized Catalonia. Continue up to the third floor, where displays explain Catalonia's industrial growth in the 19th century, life under the Franco dictatorship, and the present-day democracy. The museum offers plenty of hands-on involvement for younger visitors. Try lifting a suit of armor to discover how knights (and their horses) suffered or learn how to build a Roman arch to appreciate ancient

The vast warehouse museum building once held goods brought by sea to the nearby port.

building techniques. Visit the restaurant and terrace on the fourth floor for coffee with a dramatic view of **Port Vell** and allow time to browse in the museum store.

Plaça de Pau Vila, 3 • www.mhcat.cat • 932 254 700 • € • Closed Sun. p.m., Mon., Jan. 1 and 6, Dec. 25–26 • Metro: Barceloneta

## L'Aquàrium

**2** Instantly popular when it opened in 1995, the aquarium plunges you into a magical underwater world of 23 different exhibits. Follow a route through many kinds of seabeds and ecosystems contained in seven tropical tanks, ranging from the Great Barrier Reef to the Red Sea. Then view the comprehensive collection of Mediterranean species, the most important in the world. The highlight of this section is the vast **Oceanario,** measuring 118 feet (36 m) wide by 16.5 feet (5 m) deep, with 80 species swimming in re-creations of their natural

**Around 11,000 fish representing more than 400 species swim in the aquarium's huge tanks. Computers control the lighting to replicate natural habitats.**

habitat. A long transparent tunnel passes below this 1.05-million-gallon (4 million L) tank enhancing your sensation of swimming among the fish. It is still a surprise to come face-to-face with sharks and stingrays, while octopus, sea stars, and gilt-head bream seem less alarming. In the tropical area, creatures range from scary species such as stonefish, whose spines are 20 times more deadly than a cobra's bite, to delicate sea horses and comic clown fish, the colorful fish best known for the lead role in the movie, *Finding Nemo.* For more daring visitors the aquarium offers opportunities to swim amid the sharks (see the website for requirements, costs, and reservations).

Moll d'Espanya del Port Vell • www.aquariumbcn.com • 932 217 474 • €€€€
• Metro: Drassanes or Barceloneta

**ON THE WATERFRONT**

## GOOD **EATS**

### ■ AGUA
One of the most appealing on the waterfront, this restaurant serves modern Mediterranean dishes. Reserve a table on the terrace by the beach. **Passeig Marítim, 30, 932 251 272, €€€**

### ■ CARBALLEIRA
One of the first Galician seafood restaurants to open in Barcelona offers specialties including *centollo gallega* (spider crab) and *parillada de pescado* (assorted grilled fish). **Reina Cristina, 3, 933 101 006, €€€€**

### ■ EL VASO DE ORO
Find this long, narrow bar on a side street in Barceloneta for a cool beer. It is known for traditional tapas, such as *pebrots de Padró* (tiny green peppers) and *croquetes*. **Balboa, 7, 933 193 098, €€**

## Golondrinas

**3** Moored at the quayside, the boats *Lolita, Encarnación,* and *Maria del Carmen* wait to take passengers on a 35-minute trip around the port. Known collectively as the Golondrinas, the boats have been plying these waters since 1888, pausing only during the 1936–1939 Civil War because of a fuel shortage. Sit on the top deck of one of these old vessels and feel the cool breeze as you sail past hotel-size cruise ships, fishing boats, and a landscape of containers in the industrial port. A larger, modern catamaran with a transparent floor belowdecks travels around the port, then out to sea. This route sails the length of the waterfront past the Olympic Port to the site of the Universal Forum of Cultures 2004. On this 90-minute trip you can disembark to explore the site, now an event venue, and return on a later boat.

Moll de les Drassanes • www.lasgolondrinas.com • 934 423 106 • Port trip €€, Coast trip €€€ • Closed Jan. 1 and 6, Dec. 24–25

**The Golondrinas boats have sailed from the harbor for more than 100 years.**

## Mirador de Colom

**4** Stand a short distance away to fully appreciate Christopher Columbus atop his high monument, an iconic landmark on Barcelona's waterfront. He firmly points to the south though he sailed west from Andalucía on his voyage to find the East Indies. However, on his triumphant return he did choose to disembark in Barcelona. According to legend, he was welcomed in the **Plaça del Rei** (see pp. 54–55) by the Catholic Monarchs Ferdinand and Isabella. The sturdy cast-iron lions guarding the base make a favorite spot for photos. Walk past the crowds of young visitors on the plinth steps to see details of Columbus's story. Bronze reliefs depict scenes of his epic voyage, including the dramatic moment when Columbus arrived in America on October 12, 1492, now a national holiday in Spain.

**The towering bronze column commemorating Columbus's discovery of America is visible from across the city and marks the end of La Rambla.**

This monumental engineering feat, constructed over a seven-year period for the 1888 exhibition, extolled Catalonia's industrial progress. A plaque states that the mayor of Genoa, in Italy, attended the laying of the foundation stone because Columbus was presumed to be Genoese. Current theories, however, suggest that the explorer had Catalan origins. An elevator whizzes you to an enclosed lookout point at the top of the tower for a magnificent view of the port, church spires, and the Collserola mountains, which form a backdrop to the city.

Plaça Portal de la Pau • www.barcelonaturisme.com • 932 853 834 • € • Closed Jan. 1, Dec. 25 • Metro: Drassaness

## Museu Marítim de Barcelona

**5** See pp. 86–87.

Av. de les Drassanes • www.mmb.cat • 933 429 920 • €€ incl. visit to Santa Eulàlia • Closed Jan. 1 and 6, Dec. 25–26 • Metro: Drassanes

## Transbordador Aeri

**6** Walking toward the curvaceous **World Trade Center** at the end of the quayside, you will see the *transbordador aeri,* bright-red cable cars silently coming down from Montjuïc or crossing the harbor from Barceloneta. They dock at the top of **Torre de Jaume I,** an impressive 351-foot-high (107 m) iron tower designed by Carles Buïgas, son of the Columbus monument's architect. Board a cable car and enjoy a new perspective of the city as you soar high above the water. Disembark at the **Torre de Sant Sebastià** near the beach of the same name. Linger a while at the top of the tower to enjoy the view of the harbor and beach. At this time of day you should see the fishing fleet docking at the **Moll de Pescadors** with its landmark clock tower, once a lighthouse.

Moll de Barcelona • www.telefericodebarcelona.com • 934 304 716 • €€ • Closed Dec. 25 • Metro: Barceloneta or Drassanes

## Vila Olímpica and Port Olímpic

**7** Back on terra firma, stride out along the promenade or beach toward the Olympic Village, clearly marked by twin buildings, a new landmark on Barcelona's skyline. The first tower is the luxury **Hotel Arts,** a favorite destination for rock bands and movie stars. Woody Allen made this plush location his headquarters while filming *Vicky Cristina Barcelona* in 2007. On the street level of the hotel, the **Gran Casino** often holds concerts and shows. Some of the restaurants on this small

### SAVVY **TRAVELER**

Avoid the many restaurants clamoring for trade along the Passeig de Joan de Borbó in Barceloneta. For a more genuine dining experience, seek out bars near Barceloneta market in Plaça de la Font, or on streets such as Ginebra or Maquinista.

Bars and restaurants light up the waterside, making it a great evening destination.

stretch of beach near the casino have become all-day clubs, serving drinks during the day and well into the night.

The second tower houses offices with enviable views, near a residential area. Built on reclaimed industrial land to accommodate athletes attending the 1992 Summer Olympics, the village has become a desirable place to live, especially for enthusiastic joggers and young families who value outdoor life in the middle of the city. Its Yelmo cinema complex with 15 screens offers V.O. (original language) movies. Wander down the central boulevard, Av. d'Icària, shaded by a pergola of twisted metal and wood designed by Catalan architect Enric Miralles. The Olympic Port, crammed with yachts and a wide range of restaurants, is a popular nighttime venue: It's a good place to sip a cocktail and watch the moon rise after a long day's tour.

Vila Olímpica • Metro: Ciutadella Vila Olímpica

# Museu Marítim de Barcelona

*Visit a museum that reveals the city's maritime past and step on board a schooner in the port.*

The *Galera Reial* warship was built in the shipyard that now houses the Maritime Museum.

Discover the city's seafaring history from the medieval period to the present day in the Maritime Museum, which is set in the Drassanes Reials, formerly the royal shipyard. Since medieval times, the shipyard made the vessels that conquered territories and traded with states across the Mediterranean. The shipyard was rebuilt in 1670, in the Catalan Gothic style of the original site. The museum displays exhibits inside the building and in the courtyard. Don't miss the museum's own ship, the *Santa Eulàlia*.

## ■ Seafaring Life

In the entrance area, a model of Barcelona's 15th-century waterfront shows how important maritime activities were for the city. It includes the port area and city sites that you can see today, including the church of Santa Maria del Mar (see p. 98–99). Items from the museum's collection are displayed in rotation in the ground-floor galleries, including illustrated charts, such as an example from 1439 by Gabriel de Vallseca, and weathered but colorful ships' figureheads.

## ■ Royal Warships

Walk through into a huge space where galleys were built. Despite the soaring arches and Gothic proportions, the main area could accommodate only one ship at a time. The *Galera Reial,* built in the shipyard in 1568, was one of the largest warships of the era. A life-size reproduction shows the scale of these vessels. During combat, 236 oarsmen worked 59 oars to propel the ship.

## ■ Garden

Allow time to enjoy the peaceful garden, shaded between tall trees and the towering, buttressed walls

### SAVVY **TRAVELLER**

The museum restaurant serves a Catalan lunchtime *menú del día* (menu of the day) in an impressive setting. Sit beneath a high roof overlooking the garden pond, through the room's glass wall. Alternatively, stop for a drink or snack at tables set beside the pond. Check the museum's busy calendar, as musical events often take place in the historic **Sala Marqués de Comillas.**

of the museum. Discover exhibits from Barcelona's more recent past, including the first civil submarine in the world, the *Ictineo I* invented by Catalan Narcís Monturiol in 1859. Peep into the bridge of *Sayremar I,* a 20th-century vessel rescued by the museum in 1997; it gives a vivid idea of the day-to-day life of a mariner.

## ■ Floating Exhibit

Walk to the seafront to see the beautiful *Santa Eulàlia (Moll de la Fusta, closed Mon., Sat. a.m.),* an 1839 three-masted schooner once used for coastal trading. Restored by the museum, this popular boat's moment of pride comes on January 5 when it brings the three kings to the city (see p. 88).

Av. de les Drassanes • www.mmb.cat • 933 429 920 • €€ incl. visit to Santa Eulàlia • Closed Jan. 1 and 6, Dec. 25–26 • Metro: Drassanes

# Festivals

Catalans celebrate a range of festivals from *festes majors,* neighborhood parties, to traditional ceremonies throughout the year. Barcelonans fiercely safeguard their feast days and holidays, as an expression of their Catalan identity and as a chance to have fun. New creative influences have expanded the calender of events, and Barcelona has become a favorite venue for contemporary cultural and music festivals that attract participants from around the world.

**Months of preparation make Gràcia's festival (above) in August one of the best in the city. The Three Kings (right) bring children gifts on January 6, so their arrival in the port causes great excitement. Many Spanish children receive gifts at Epiphany, not Christmas.**

### A Calendar of Celebrations

Religious feast days usually offer a colorful spectacle; on the eve of Epiphany ( January 5), Els Reis, the three kings, arrive magically in the port at twilight aboard the schooner *Santa Eulàlia* (see p. 87). The kings travel up Via Laietana on elaborate floats, while their pages throw candy to eager crowds. Carnival time in February features more processions, such as the grand *ruas,* when everyone dresses up. Also, in the week before Carnival, children wear costumes to school. Love is in the air on St. George's Day, April 23, when Catalans celebrate their patron saint in a romantic exchange of roses and books (see p. 73). Unique to Catalonia, the spectacular *l'ou com balla*—"the dancing egg"—occurs in May or June to celebrate the feast of Corpus Christi. Following an old tradition, an egg seems to "dance" atop the spout of a fountain decorated with flowers. Do not miss this sight in the patios of the Barri Gòtic, notably the Casa de l'Ardiaca, the cathedral cloisters, or the Palau del Lloctinent in the **Plaça del Rei** (see pp. 54–55).

## Festes Majors

People travel from other countries to join in La Mercè, the city's annual party or *festa major* (see p. 72–73). But local *festes majors* are held in neighborhoods throughout the year. From Barceloneta to Sants, the party ingredients include *sardana* dancing, processions, and fireworks.

## Culture & Music

Artists at the Grec Summer Festival of theater, music, and dance enjoy performing at the **Grec amphitheater** on Montjuïc and in the old town squares. In June the Sónar International Festival of Advanced Music pulls in trendy crowds, and the International Jazz Festival boasts locations such as the **Palau de la Música Catalana** (see pp. 96–97).

## FESTIVAL **FOOD**

Celebrations include traditional festive foods.

**Carnaval** Before Lent begins, indulge in *botifarra d'ou,* a rich sausage.

**Easter** Godparents give their godchildren a *Mona,* a decorated cake at Easter. Go to Escribà *(La Rambla, 83)* for chocolate samples.

**Epiphany** *Tortell de Reis,* a marzipan pastry, comes with a paper crown at Epiphany; hidden inside are a dried bean and a toy king. If you find the king, you wear the crown, but if you bite on the bean, you have to buy next year's *tortell.*

# Beaches

Barcelona offers visitors an appealing mix of urban sightseeing and beach life. After taking in the best of the city, head to one of Barcelona's seven beaches to unwind. Alternatively, if you are looking for a quieter place, take a short train ride along the coast to one of the many coves and resorts.

■ SANT SEBASTIÀ

The locals' most popular beach lies at the southernmost end of Barceloneta. Its name refers to the Banys Sant Sebastià, one of several 19th-century swimming baths that stood on the site. Preparations for the 1992 Summer Olympics cleared the area, providing the city with new beaches fully equipped with showers, public conveniences, and lifeguards. Recent building work for the towering 26-story **W** hotel *(Plaça de la Rosa dels Vents, 1, 932 952 800)* gave the beach a sheltered swimming bay. The bars under the hotel add glamour and by sunset throb with cool music. The hotel's own bar, **Salt** *(Passeig del Mare Nostrum, 932 952 819)*, offers an opportunity to sip a cocktail with your toes in the sand. For delicious rice dishes and salads served in chic, Mediterranean style try **Pez Vela** *(Passeig del Mare Nostrum, 19–21, 932 216 317)*.

■ MAR BELLA

One of the newest beaches located beyond the Olympic Port, Mar Bella feels refreshingly far from the city bustle. Only a short walk from Poblenou Metro, the grass-covered dunes and laid-back crowd create an ambience that has made it a favorite beach with nudists. The family-friendly **Parc de Poblenou,** behind the promenade, offers a skateboard half-pipe and Ping-Pong tables. By nightfall **El Chiringuito de la Mar Bella** beach bar gets into its stride, drawing a multicultural party crowd. The neighboring bar **Relevant** serves tapas all day and features a program of events, from circuses to concerts. Check out the village atmosphere of Rambla de Poblenou, a boulevard lined with cafés and bars, situated in the former industrial district. **El Tio Che** *(Rambla de Poblenou, 44)* has been serving *orxata,* a thirst-quenching drink made from tiger nuts, for more than 100 years.

ON THE WATERFRONT

**Barcelona's beaches, created from an industrial area, are now popular with locals and visitors.**

### ◼ BADALONA

A busy town in its own right, Badalona's waterfront has the atmosphere of a resort with its promenade, palm trees, and pretty 19th-century villas. Only 20 minutes from Plaça de Catalunya on a RENFE mainline train, Badalona provides a nearby alternative to the city beaches. Walk a few hundred yards north from the station to escape the town's crowds. The farther you wander, the more peaceful the area becomes.

### ◼ SITGES

Well known for its artistic past (see pp. 170–171) and its recent gay scene, this attractive, whitewashed seaside town oozes charm. Only 40 minutes by RENFE train from Passeig de Gràcia or Sants station, Sitges has a distinctive atmosphere; you may feel as though you have traveled much farther south. A string of golden beaches runs from **Sant Bartomeu i Santa Tecla** church that stands on the headland. Child-friendly shallow water and brightly colored sun loungers and parasols all contribute to a relaxing break from the city. For a perfect day follow the locals and stop at lunchtime for a delicious paella in the traditional beachside hotel **La Santa María** *(Passeig de la Ribera, 52, 938 940 999),* followed by a siesta on your sun lounger.

# La Ribera

In La Ribera, traditional local shops and bars cohabit with stylish boutiques and chic eateries. This fashionably eclectic part of the city lies to the north of Via Laietana, the road that cuts through the old town with the Barri Gòtic on the other side. A strong medieval flavor permeates the labyrinthine lanes built in the 13th century, when merchants returned from overseas ventures to settle in La Ribera, a neighborhood that used to be closer to the sea. By the end of the 14th century, merchants had built the palaces lining Montcada, now home to the Museu Picasso, and the church of Santa Maria del Mar, a jewel of Catalan Gothic style. The area's fortune turned in 1714, when Philip V forced Barcelona to submit to his rule and destroyed much of the area to build a citadel. Eventually torn down, the citadel made way for Ciutadella Park and zoo. Near this open space lies the trendy rejuventated area around Passeig del Born. Explore the converted commercial buildings here, such as the Born Cultural Center, once an indoor market.

◀ **The faded facades of apartment buildings stand beside cool restaurants and unique shops in colorful La Ribera.**

# La Ribera

*Architectural gems, the city zoo, a modern master, and unique bars and shops make La Ribera a vibrant and varied place to visit.*

**❶ Palau de la Música Catalana** (see pp. 96–97) The elaborate *modernista* concert hall opened in 1908. Today it hosts a busy program of classical concerts, jazz, and flamenco. Take Verdaguer i Callís, turn left on Sant Pere Més Baix and then right on Freixures.

**❷ Mercat de Santa Caterina** (see p. 97) Feast your eyes in this busy market with a designer edge. Exit near the remains of a convent at the back and go down Sant Jacint, turn left into Corders, and then right at a Romanesque chapel. Cross Princesa to reach Montcada.

**❸ Museu Picasso** (see pp. 102–105) Five medieval palaces are an impressive home for this huge collection of Picasso's work. Temporary exhibitions on related themes also take place here. Wander down Montcada to see buildings of the medieval boom period, then walk along Sombrerers to the main entrance of the church.

PLAÇA D'URQUINAONA

Urquinaona

C. DE TRAFALGAR

VIA      LAIETANA

PLAÇA D'ANTONI MAURA

AVINGUDA DE F. CAMBÓ

Palau de la Música Catalana ❶

CARRER SANT PERE MÉS ALT

CARRER SANT PERE MÉS MITJÀ

CARRER SANT PERE MÉS BAIX

LA RIBERA

Mercat de Santa Caterina ❷

RONDA DE SANT PERE

CARRER DE TRAFALGAR

PLAÇA DE SANT PERE

CORDERS

...ERC

Arc de Triomf

AV. VILANOVA

C. DELS ALMOGÀVERS

PASSEIG DE LLUÍS COMPANYS

PASSEIG DE LLUÍS COMPANYS

C. DE BUENAVENTURA MUÑOZ

**4 Santa Maria del Mar**
(see pp. 98–99) The striking facade and soaring interior of this church embody Catalan Gothic architecture: This is said to be the most beautiful church in Barcelona. Take the side door into the Plaça Fossar de les Moreres, a memorial square to the martyrs of the 1714 siege, then head to Passeig del Born.

**5 Passeig del Born** (see p. 99) The narrow medieval streets leading off Passeig del Born contain a wealth of small fashion boutiques. After meandering, return to the Passeig, once the site of tournaments, now lined with cocktail bars and cafés, and continue to the impressive building at the end.

**6 Born Centre Cultural** (see p. 100) This historic former market is now a cultural center. Take the cobbled street, Ribera, and cross Passeig de Picasso. Notice Tàpies's "Homage to Picasso" in a transparent cube just outside the park entrance.

**7 Parc de la Ciutadella** (see pp. 100–101) This large park contains the zoo, the Catalan Parliament, and some *modernista* buildings. The park provides a great space to relax or play sports, especially on the weekend.

## LA RIBERA

**LA RIBERA DISTANCE: 2.8 MILES (4.5 KM)**
**TIME: APPROX. 7 HOURS METRO START: URQUINAONA**

## Palau de la Música Catalana

**1** This "palace of music" has a new extension and entrance in Palau de la Música, but start your visit on the adjacent street, Sant Pere Més Alt. Look up to appreciate the glorious facade of the original entrance with its combination of red bricks, colored glass, and pastel ceramic tiles decorating the columns on the first floor and the former ticket offices at street level. A leading light in the *modernisme* (Catalan modernism) movement (see pp. 122–123) and a contemporary of Gaudí, Lluis Domènech i Montaner designed the concert hall for a choral society, the Orfeó Català. The modern extension by Catalan architect Tusquets, which houses the chamber concert hall, continues the redbrick and glass theme. At the new entrance, an outdoor terrace makes a perfect spot for breakfast under the baton of the statue of Lluís Millet, founder of the Orfeó. Or, to absorb the decorative details of this opulent space, enjoy your coffee

A sunburst skylight illuminates the 2,000-seat auditorium of the Palau de la Música Catalana.

in the original foyer bar. You can walk through the bar to see the the old entrance hall, but to see the main auditorium you need to buy a concert ticket or take a guided tour (half-hourly 10 a.m.–3:30 p.m.). Worth the price of either ticket, the auditorium's extravagant *modernista* (Catalan modernist) decoration brings together the main decorative arts of the time: ironwork, ceramics, and glass.

Palau de la Música, 4–6 • www.palaumusica.cat • 932 957 200 • Tours daily • €€€€
• Metro: Urquinaona

## Mercat de Santa Caterina

**2** Emerge from the dark, narrow streets, with laundry hanging overhead, into broad Avinguda de Francesc Cambó bustling with the noise of a typical neighborhood marketplace. Santa Caterina market, built on the site of a former convent in 1848, was completely reconstructed in 2005 by star Catalan architect Enric Miralles, who transformed it into Barcelona's first designer market. A roof mosaic of

**The entrance to Santa Caterina creates a dynamic centerpiece to this local market.**

325,000 tiles in bright colors represents the fruits and vegetables on sale under the undulating structure supported by twisted metal struts. Enter through the arched facade, all that remains of the original market, and wander through the alleyways between stalls displaying exquisite seasonal produce from the Mediterranean and farther afield, from artichokes and wild mushrooms to squid and lobsters. A good place to stop for lunch, the market offers a few choices; sample excellent Mediterranean food, as well as some Asian dishes, at the fashionable **Cuines Santa Caterina** restaurant *(932 689 918)*. In contrast, join fishwives and office workers for a good-value typical Catalan lunch, a *menú del día*, at **Bar Joan** *(Stand 108, 933 106 150)*.

Av. de Francesc Cambó, 16 • www.mercatsantacaterina.com • 933 195 740
• Closed Sun. • Metro: Urquinaona or Jaume I

## Museu Picasso

**3** See pp. 102–105.

Montcada, 15–23 • www.museupicasso.bcn.cat • 932 563 000 • €€€
• Closed Mon., Jan. 1, May 1, June 24, Dec. 25–26 • Metro: Jaume I

## Santa Maria del Mar

**4** Stand in the Plaça de Santa Maria with your back to the 1402 fountain, said to be the oldest in Barcelona, and look up at the handsome, sturdy facade of the "cathedral of the sea." Admire the two octagonal bell towers that taper into the sky on either side of a rose window. Don't miss the glimpses of everyday medieval life in motifs such as two porters on the main doors, placed in honor of the neighborhood workers who built the church. The relatively short construction period (1329–1384) means the architecture has a rare uniformity of style—churches often took centuries to build. Step inside the church to gaze at the sheer majesty of the spacious, lofty interior. Tall slim pillars soar upward to the roof; the spans between them, at 42 feet (13 m), are the widest of any Gothic church in Europe. The slender columns group closer together around the altar to delineate the sacred area. Berenguer de Montagut, the 14th-century master builder responsible for this ambitious project, was known for keeping interior decoration and partitions to a minimum. A fire during the Civil War in 1936 only added to this minimalism by ridding the church of ornate features, resulting in the uncluttered simplicity of the interior we see

**An earthquake shattered the original rose window, but a 15th-century restoration renewed its glory.**

today. For a truly uplifting experience try to catch a concert here, such as "The Messiah" usually performed in December, or Mozart's "Requiem" sung at Easter time.

Plaça de Santa Maria, 1 • www.stamariadelmar.org
• 933 102 390 • Closed 1:30 p.m.–4:30 p.m. • Metro:
Jaume I or Barceloneta

## Passeig del Born

**5** The Passeig del Born, a rectangular esplanade, acts as the unofficial center of the area known as the Born, the part of La Ribera southeast of Princesa. The neighborhood attracts people as much for its individual shops and vibrant nightlife, as for its cultural legacy. Luckily, most of these establishments have remained small, independent, and attractive, adding to the charms of the neighborhood. The fashion boutiques are almost like small art galleries. Whichever turn you take off the Passeig into the labyrinth of streets, you will find treats, often in quirky, renovated spaces. Down picturesque Vidrieria, **Anna Povo** *(No. 11)*, a Barcelona designer, sells comfortable but stylish women's clothes in natural fabrics. On the other side of the Passeig, **Cortana** *(Flassaders, 41)* offers elegant ball gowns and wedding gear designed by Rosa Esteva, who hails from the island of Mallorca. On the same street, just behind Museu Picasso, **RooM** *(No. 31)* has women's fashion by Catalan designer Maria Roch. Next door, **Èstro** *(No. 33)* specializes in luxurious Italian leather for men and women. An emporium of vintage clothes, gadgets, and retro music, **Loisaida** *(No. 42)* also sells independent clothes labels. Back on the Passeig, **Tascón** *(No. 8)* has a large range of shoes and specializes in Spanish designs from famous makes such as Camper and Vialis.

Passeig del Born • Metro: Jaume I or Barceloneta

## GOOD **EATS**

### ■ CAL PEP
At this popular restaurant the bar is the only place to be for the view of the dexterous cooks conjuring up Mediterranean delights, such as *xipirons amb cigrons* (baby squid with chick peas) or *cloïsses amb pernil* (clams with Serrano ham). Or order from a selection of more than 70 tapas. **Plaça de les Olles, 8, 933 107 961, €€€**

### ■ LA VINYA DEL SENYOR
In a privileged location with an inviting terrace at the foot of the steps of Santa Maria del Mar, this *vinoteca* (wine bar) offers an interesting range of unusual Spanish and international wines by the glass. Choose some *platillos* (small dishes) and tapas to complement the wine. **Plaça de Santa Maria del Mar, 5, 933 103 379, €€**

LA RIBERA

**LA RIBERA**

## SAVVY **TRAVELER**

La Diada, the Catalan national holiday on September 11, commemorates the city's surrender to Felipe V (see Born Centre Cultural). Beginning with a ceremony in the Parc de la Ciutadella with the local dignitaries and police in dress uniform singing the national anthem, it usually ends near Santa Maria del Mar church.

## Born Centre Cultural

**6** This fine wrought iron building took its inspiration from northern European constructions of the time, such as the Eiffel Tower. These buildings twisted metal into modern feats of engineering. The Born opened as Barcelona's central market in 1876, but it closed more than 40 years ago, before being renovated as a cultural and historical center—Born CC. Inside the center, follow the walkways over the ruins of medieval houses discovered under the building's foundations. The houses had been destroyed to make way for the citadel, after the seige and fall of Barcelona to Felipe V on September 11, 1714, a day now known as the Diada, the Catalan national day. Symbolically, the new Born CC opened on September 11, 2013, to start the celebrations for the 300th anniversary of the city's defeat. An exhibition in the **Sala Villarroel** displays some 2,800 objects found in the ruins, including household utensils, ceramics, and 300 cannonballs from the siege. Exhibits and audiovisuals show the heroic resistance of Barcelona's citizens during that tragic period. After seeing the exhibits, walk through the building, under the original vast tiled roof, to the Ciutadella Park.

Plaça Comercial, 12• www.elborncentrecultural.cat •932 566 851 • €€ • Closed Mon., Jan. 1, May 1, June 24, Dec. 25 • Metro: Jaume I or Barceloneta

## Parc de la Ciutadella

**7** This much loved park takes its name from the former military citadel that once housed 8,000 Spanish troops on the site. Given back to the city in 1869, the area became the grounds for the 1888 International Exhibition before being turned into a park. Walk past magnificent palm trees and magnolias to see the glorious exhibition buildings—the **Umbracle,** home to tropical plants, the **Hivernacle,** a *modernista* greenhouse, and the redbrick **Castell dels Tres Dragons,**

designed by Lluis Domènech i Montaner as the exhibition restaurant. Make your way along shady paths to the **Cascada,** a monumental waterfall and fountain with an open-air café. Next, rent a boat on the larger lake to row among the geese, then wander over to the **Parlament de Catalunya,** where politicians debate the order of the day. The pond in front of the building contains a copy of a famous sculpture **"El Desconsol"** ("Desolation") by Catalan Josep Llimona: View the original in the Museu Nacional (see pp. 168–169). A major attraction, the **Barcelona Zoo,** founded in 1892, occupies half the park (see pp. 34–35). The park closes at sunset, a good time to return to the Born and choose a buzzing place for a cocktail or dinner.

Entrances in Passeig de Picasso and Passeig de Pujades • Metro: Arc de Triomf, Barceloneta, Jaume I, or Ciutadella Vila Olímpica

LA RIBERA

A network of paths crisscrosses Parc de la Ciutadella, leadng walkers past trees and fountains.

LA RIBERA

# Museu Picasso

*A series of medieval palaces exhibit Picasso's early work,*
*much of which was painted when he lived in Barcelona.*

**The Catalan Gothic architecture of the palaces makes a distinctive setting for the museum.**

The acclaimed Barcelona Museu Picasso opened in 1963, the first of five museums in Europe devoted entirely to the work of this seminal 20th-century artist. The museum charts Pablo Ruiz y Picasso's relationship with Barcelona through the world's largest collection of his early paintings and drawings. Gain an insight into Picasso's formative years before viewing pieces from the Blue Period. The museum contains later works, too, including an exhaustive study of "Las Meninas" from 1957, and his lesser known ceramics.

## ■ PALATIAL SURROUNDINGS

The museum occupies five medieval palaces on Montcada, Barcelona's grand medieval street, that had fallen into disrepair by the 20th century. Initially, the renovated **Palau Aguilar** (*No. 15*) held the collection, but it expanded over many years with donations of work, notably from the artist himself in 1970. Now the museum seamlessly connects **Palau Baró de Castellet** (*No. 17*), **Palau Meca** (*No. 19*), **Casa Mauri** (*No. 21*), and **Palau Finestres** (*No. 23*). Constructed between the 13th and 15th centuries, the wide, open entrance to each building leads into a courtyard with a grand staircase to the first floor. Take time to observe some wonderful details of Catalan Gothic architecture, as well as features from later periods including a *modernista* spiral staircase.

## ■ FROM MÁLAGA TO BARCELONA

Starting in Palau Meca, follow the chronological order of the collection. Born in Malaga in 1881, Picasso's family moved to Barcelona in 1895. The first rooms of the museum show Picasso's extraordinary early skills and technique, including small accomplished oil paintings on wood such as the **"Casa del Camp"**

## IN **THE KNOW**

When the museum opened just over 50 years ago, it was called the Sabartés Collection. Jaume Sabartés, Picasso's close friend and secretary, had helped to establish the museum and donated his own collection. The museum could not bear Picasso's name because he had taken a public stance against the Franco regime. Communist all his life, the artist refused to return to Spain while the dictator lived and, since Franco outlived him by two years, he never saw his museum.

("Country House"), made when he was only 12 years old. Between the ages of 13 and 14, Picasso produced pieces with extraordinary depth, such as the oil painting **"Home amb boina"** ("Man in a Beret") and a self-portrait. Photographs taken at the time (see p. 104) show how well Picasso captured the intense vitality in his dark eyes. The masterly, very touching watercolor of his father, **"Retrat del pare de l'artista,"** seems to come from the hand of a mature artist. His father featured as a model in many paintings, including **"Primera Comunió"** ("First Communion"), which appeared in a public exhibition. Observing the work's classical style, you would never imagine Picasso would become a founder of the Cubist movement.

**LA RIBERA**

### ■ CLASSICISM TO ABSTRACT

A turning point in Picasso's early work was **"Ciència i Caritat"** ("Science and Charity"), which won an award in 1897 in Madrid, where Picasso studied briefly. See this large canvas in room three and notice the palpable suffering in the work that reflects the social realism of the time. Details such as damp stains on the walls show the poverty in which the sick woman lives. Do not miss the display of the young Picasso's sketchbooks: These show his early talent.

**A photograph of Picasso taken in Barcelona when he was 14 years old**

Having eventually rejected academic training, Picasso returned to Barcelona and mingled with the avant-garde artists and writers who used to meet in **Els Quatre Gats bar** (see p. 170). See his distinctive style emerge in room four, where Picasso's portraits of artists in Els Quatre Gats group, as well as his younger sister Lola and his friend Jaume Sabartés, hang.

Views from windows are a recurrent theme in Picasso's work. One of the earliest, **"El carrer de la Riera de Sant Joan,"** shows a scene from his studio in Riera de Sant Joan, a street later demolished to build Via Laietana. Painted in 1900, this work shows the first signs of Picasso's evolving abstract style. Watch out for the small sketches of bullfighting, some made during summer visits to Málaga and others marking the opening of Les Arenes bullring in **Plaça d'Espanya** (see p. 162). Picassso captures the movement and atmosphere of a bullfight in a few dramatic strokes.

### ■ PARIS 1900–1901

Picasso made his first trip to Paris in 1900 and spent many years traveling between Paris and Barcelona, before settling in southern France. Rooms five to seven focus on his first time in

France with paintings of Parisian bohemian life and a decadent theatrical world, as in **"L'Espera. Margot"** ("The Wait. Margot"), a colorful portrait of a morphine addict or prostitute. The influences of painters in Paris, such as Van Gogh and Toulouse-Lautrec, may be seen in **"La fi del número"** ("The End of the Number").

### ■ BLUE & ROSE PERIODS

Works from Picasso's Blue Period in room eight depict poor, socially outcast characters in shades of blue as in **"Desemparats"** ("Helpless"). Quite sparsely represented in the museum, these paintings echo the artist's own depression, which lifted with the Rose Period. The subtle tones in the portrait of Benedetta Bianco, painted in 1905, indicate the change of style, shown in room nine. In the next two rooms, see the new subjects and an interest in neo-classicism that emerged particulary after Picasso's trip to Barcelona, in 1917. Here, he worked with Diaghilev's Ballets Russes, who performed "Parade" in the Liceu on La Rambla. **"Arlequí"** ("Harlequin"), painted during this visit, was the first painting the artist gave to Barcelona, in 1919.

### ■ LAS MENINAS & BEYOND

The next area, in rooms twelve to fourteen, take you to 1957 with **"Las Meninas."** Here you will see Picasso's prolific study of the 17th–century Diego Velázquez masterpiece of the same title. Forty-four colorful paintings line the walls of three beautifully restored rooms.

A portrait of Picasso's last wife, Jacqueline, presides over a room housing paintings of the dovecote at his French home. These are complemented by photographs of the couple. In 1982, Jacqueline gave her personal collection of forty-one pieces of Picasso's ceramics to the museum. The influence of the Mediterranean is evident on the bright ceramics featuring fish and animals. The final rooms include examples of Picasso's prints and linocuts, many using the latest techniques of the time.

The museum exhibits change regularly, so you may see different pieces in a different order or in other rooms. Do explore the museum store, full of postcards and volumes on this groundbreaking artist who straddled the 19th and 20th centuries.

Montcada, 15–23 • www.museupicasso.bcn.cat • 932 563 000 • €€€ • Closed Mon., Jan. 1, May 1, June 24, Dec. 25–26 • Metro: Jaume I

# Catalan Cusine

Michelin stars fire the culinary rivalry between the restaurants of Catalonia and the Basque Country. But it is the quality of everyday cooking that led one food writer to declare that Catalan cooking is Europe's last great culinary secret. With more than 3,000 restaurants in Barcelona to choose from, dozens of markets selling fresh local produce, and excellent grocery stores, getting to know the local fare will be an enjoyable experience.

LA RIBERA

Spanish olive oil (above) originates from many regions, including Catalonia. Olive oil features in the popular *pa amb tomàquet* and in most tapas. Fish and rice dishes are popular in Barcelona, and freshly prepared *paella* (right) is often served at fiestas.

## From Land and Sea

Catalan food uses the freshest ingredients from the mountains and valleys of the area, as well as seafood from the coast. The secret to the best flavors lies in the seasonality of the produce. Look for restaurants serving *cuina del mercat*—fresh from the market. In the fall, try *bolets* (wild mushrooms) grilled with garlic and parsley or in rich stews. In the spring, sample *calçots,* a type of large scallion cooked on an open fire, often outdoors, and served with a delicious sauce made from pounded garlic, hazelnuts, almonds, tomatoes, and *ñora* pepper. Some dishes, known as *mar i muntanya,* combine produce from the land and the sea: *pollastre amb escamarlans* (chicken with langoustines) or *peus de porc i bogavant* (pigs' trotters with lobster).

## A Catalan Speciality

Olive oil and tomatoes, fundamental ingredients in Mediterranean cooking, combine in the quintessential Catalan dish, *pa amb tomàquet:* crispy fresh bread rubbed with tomato, a trickle of virgin olive oil, and a sprinkling of salt. Found everywhere, from corner bars to fancy restaurants, *pa amb tomàquet* (literally "bread and tomatoes") makes a healthy starter or an accompaniment to grilled meats, *truita* (omelette), *embotits* (cured meats), or *formatge de cabra* (goat cheese).

## Sunday Lunch

Eating in Barcelona is about socializing. Workers often eat lunch together, and on Sundays, members of extended families and friends gather for a leisurely meal. Sunday lunch may be eaten at home or in a local restaurant. It is followed by a *postre* (dessert) bought from a pastry shop and may be accompanied by *cava*, sparkling wine made on the outskirts of Barcelona.

## BARCELONA **MEALS**

"Do as the Catalans" for an authentic culinary experience in Barcelona. Breakfast on *cafè amb llet* (milky coffee) or a sturdy *esmorzar de forquilla* (fork breakfast), such as poached egg with baby squid, washed down with wine. Join office workers at 2 p.m. for a *menú del día,* an excellent value three-course set-lunch, including a drink for 10–15 euros. Squeeze in a snack, a *berenar* (hot chocolate and a pastry), around 6 p.m. if you dare. Light tapas and a beer will fill the gap until dinner, which usually starts at 9 p.m.

LA RIBERA

# Shopping

Barcelona's high-quality shopping caters to all tastes, ranging from upscale fashion to handicrafts, exclusive boutiques to large malls, and antique markets to traditional stores. Unusual locations, such as *modernista* houses, medieval lanes, or seaside spaces, add an extra dimension to the pleasure of shopping in the city.

■ MARKETS

One of the most stylish of the city's municipal food markets, La Ribera's Mercat de Santa Caterina (see p. 97), offers the finest olive oils, vinegar, and salt at **Olisoliva** *(Stand 153, www .olisoliva.com, 932 681 472)*. Search the outer edge of the market for earthenware cooking pots sold in traditional shops. In Barri Gòtic, the cathedral esplanade hosts a huge Christmas market, **Fira de Santa Llúcia,** where you can buy decorations and gifts. In El Raval, the **Mercat Obert del Raval** *(Rambla del Raval, Sat. and Sun.)* is where young designers sell their stylish handmade creations, such as clothes, hats, jewelry, and bags. Try the mint tea and Arab pastries in the area selling Moroccan goods. The September fiesta of La Mercè near Passeig de Gràcia coincides with a two-week fair selling antique and modern books, **Fira del Llibre**. Near La Sagrada Família, **Els**

**Encants** *(Plaça de les Glòries, Mon., Wed., Fri., and Sat.)* flea market has become an institution where haggling is essential.

■ FROM THE TOP

Showcases for top Spanish designers line Passeig de Gràcia, the elegant boulevard of the Eixample district. Discover **Adolfo Domínguez** *(No. 32)*, the man who made wrinkled linen fashionable, **Armand Basi** *(No. 49)* for smart casual fashion, or **Loewe**'s luxury leather goods displayed in Casa Lleó Morera's *modernista* splendor *(No. 35)*. The street also features international labels, including **Chanel** *(No. 70)* and **Burberry** *(No. 56)*.

■ DISTINCTIVE STYLE

A more relaxed atmosphere prevails in the wide parallel street, Rambla de Catalunya, epitomized in **Antonio Miró** *(Rambla de Catalunya, 125)*. King of a wave of Catalan fashion in

LA RIBERA

**Enjoy the experience of shopping in Passeig de Gràcia's *modernista* buildings.**

the 1980s, Miró's new concept store offers a chill-out space at the back. His simple, stylish lines in clothes extend to ranges of accessories and eco-furniture. Interior design emporium **Vinçon** *(Passeig de Gràcia, 96)*, housed in Ramon Casas' home (see p. 170), offers inspirational ideas from corkscrews to designer furniture, as well as having a great view of the back of Gaudí's La Pedrera. Find boutiques selling lesser known designers in the Gràcia area, such as the feminine clothes of **Lydia Delgado** *(Minerva, 21)*, or try **Camiseria Pons** *(Gran de Gràcia, 49)* for a select range of labels in an original 1900 setting.

■ TRADITIONAL & ANTIQUE

Family-run stores can still be found in most neighborhoods. In Barri Gòtic, find fans galore at **Alonso** *(Santa Anna, 27)* or classical and modern rope-soled shoes made on the premises at **La Manual Alpargatera** *(Avinyó, 7)*. Seek out the exquisite antique shops behind dusty facades in the Gothic quarter streets of Palla and Sant Sever. Stalls in the Thursday antique market, **Mercat Gòtic,** in the cathedral square, sell a less pricey range of goods, from cameras to lace nightgowns. Near Passeig de Gràcia, **Guantes Victoriano** *(Mallorca, 195)* has a vast selection of gloves; if you cannot find the right color or material they will make you a pair.

PASSEIG DE GRÀCIA

Mediterranean Sea

# Passeig de Gràcia

The broad avenues of Passeig de Gràcia and Rambla de Catalunya form the elegant central section of the Eixample district. In the early 20th century, the wealthy Catalan bourgeoisie and their star architects Antoni Gaudí, Domènech i Montaner, and Puig i Cadalfalch vied with each other to build the most striking houses, creating an open-air museum of masterpieces in this district, which is also known as Quadrat d'Or (Golden Square). Today, this buzzy area abounds with glamorous shops, sophisticated art galleries, high-end hotels, and designer homes. In the 19th century, town planner, Ildefons Cerdà, designed a grid-based extension to the old city, joining it to outlying villages, including Gràcia located at the top of Passeig de Gràcia. Now a residential neighborhood with trendy bars and restaurants, Gràcia retains a villagey atmosphere. Its pretty squares, haphazard streets, and bohemian feel provide a striking contrast to the grandeur of the Eixample.

PASSEIG DE GRÀCIA

112 Neighborhood Walk

120 In Depth:
Fundació
Antoni Tàpies

122 Distinctly Barcelona:
Modernisme

124 Best Of:
Coffee & Cava

◀ **Gaudí's Casa Batlló stops the crowds. The columns, made of sandstone from Montjuïc, suggest the shape of human bones.**

# Passeig de Gràcia

*Tree-lined boulevards, sophisticated shops, and the best modernista buildings in town make this an elegant area.*

**6 La Pedrera (Casa Milà)** (see pp. 118–119) Curving around the corner of Passeig de Gràcia stands Casa Milà, a Gaudí apartment building. Built between 1906 and 1912, the astonishing building shocked people when it opened. Continue up Passeig de Gràcia across Diagonal, through the Jardins de Salvador Espriu to Gran de Gràcia. Turn right onto Goya, through Plaça de la Vila de Gràcia and on to Plaça del Sol.

**7 Gràcia** (see p. 119) This lively former village retains its local atmosphere in squares such as Plaça del Sol. The restaurants and bars provide the perfect starting point for a night out.

**5 Rambla de Catalunya** (see p. 117) This peaceful boulevard echoes its refined surroundings and smart residents. Stroll along the central walkway lined with pavement cafés and stop for lunch. Then return to Passeig de Gràcia, through Passatge de la Concepció, one of the Eixample's typical mews-style passageways.

**4 Fundació Antoni Tàpies**

(see pp. 120–121) This Catalan artist set up the foundation to exhibit his own work and other contemporary art. Admire the first *modernista* building in Barcelona, then take a few steps along Aragó to Rambla de Catalunya.

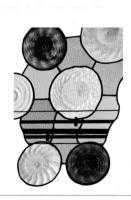

**3 Casa Batlló & Illa de la Discòrdia**

(see pp. 116–117) The block (*illa*) between this corner and the next street, Aragó, earned the name "Block of Discord" because of its contrasting buildings. Turn left onto Aragó.

**2 Consell de Cent Art Galleries**

(see p. 115) Catch up on new trends in national and international art by walking along this street, lined with private art galleries. Return to Passeig de Gràcia and turn left.

**1 Plaça de Catalunya** (see pp. 114–115) This large square is the symbolic and geographical center of the city, marking the divide between the old town and the 19th-century Eixample neighborhood. From its northern corner walk up Passeig de Gràcia to the junction of Consell de Cent and turn left.

**PASSEIG DE GRÀCIA DISTANCE: 2.2 MILES (3.5 KM)**
**TIME: APPROX. 7 HOURS  METRO START: CATALUNYA OR URQUINAONA**

## Plaça de Catalunya

**1** Breakfast in **Café Zurich** *(Plaça de Catalunya, 1)* provides a great view of this busy central square, where tourists arriving from the airport meet locals rushing to work. A hub for public transportation, Plaça de Catalunya contains the airport bus terminus, the starting point for the city tour bus, and the main tourist office. The open central space, decorated with a mosaic star and bordered with equestrian statues and fountains, attracts kids chasing pigeons and picnicking families. At night, boisterous teenagers meet to hit the nightlife, and couples sit under the statue of Macià, a former president of the Generalitat. Josep Maria Subirachs, who sculpted this angular work, also made the additions to **La Sagrada Família** church (see pp. 136–139). The large buildings surrounding the square, now shops, banks, and hotels, have been part of historic events—the Apple Store was the Socialist party headquarters in the Civil War. Recent additions

Plaça de Catalunya was designed in the 1920s, with graceful statues and cooling fountains.

include the El Triangle shopping center and a branch of El Corte Inglés, Spain's leading department store. Enjoy the walk up Passeig de Gràcia noticing the hexagonal tiles of the sidewalk, designed by Gaudí for the Casa Batlló but never used there.

Plaça de Catalunya • Metro: Catalunya or Urquinaona

## SAVVY **TRAVELER**

Save hours waiting in line by purchasing tickets online for La Sagrada Família, Casa Batlló, La Pedrera, Museu Picasso, or the tour of the Palau de la Música. Follow the instructions on the website for each attraction. Usually you can either print a ticket or collect one from any branch of La Caixa bank that has a ServiCaixa machine.

## Consell de Cent Art Galleries

**2** This classic Eixample street, where residential properties alternate with office buildings, has a larger concentration of art galleries than any other neighborhood. Exhibitions change regularly in establishments such as **Sala Dalmau** *(No. 349)*, reflecting the pulse of the contemporary art scene. Founded in 1979, this gallery shows avant-garde art from the early 20th century to the present day. Of note are the architect Le Corbusier and Torres García, the Uruguayan constructivist, who fraternized with the Els Quatre Gats group (see p. 104).

**Galeria Carles Taché** *(No. 290)* shows a broad range of artists: from Spanish Eduardo Arroyo and Antonio Saura, to Catalan Joan Brossa, founder (with Tàpies) of the Dau al Set art group. Brossa's art can be seen around Barcelona—in front of the cathedral are six large sculpted letters that spell BARCINO, the Roman name of the city. Irish-American painter Sean Scully, British sculptor Tony Cragg, and British artist Cornelia Parker all belong to this gallery. Pop into **Eude** *(No. 278)* to see modern prints, photography, and installations, or **Àmbit Galeria d'Art** *(No. 282)* to catch leading lights of the Catalan art world, including Guinovart, Ràfols-Casamada, or Josep Maria Codina. Most galleries are open 10 a.m.–2 p.m. and 5 p.m.–8:30 p.m. and close on Sundays. Thursday evening is the traditional time for openings, so swing by to mingle with art lovers over a glass of wine.

Consell de Cent• Metro: Passeig de Gràcia or Catalunya

**PASSEIG DE GRÀCIA**

## Casa Batlló & Illa de la Discòrdia

**3** Key architects of the *modernisme* movement designed houses in a range of new styles for wealthy bourgeois clients on this *illa,* a typical Eixample block. Ordinary 19th-century buildings were renovated to create three outstanding houses. On the corner stands the delicately ornate **Casa Lleó Morera** *(No. 35)* by Lluís Domènech i Montaner. It's currently closed to the public, but peep into the entrance and admire the colorful ceramic tiles and sculpted stonework. Chocolate maker Antoni Amatller, commissioned Puig i Cadafalch to create **Casa Amatller** *(No. 41)* in his neo-Gothic style, a historical reference often seen in *modernisme* and here mixed with Flemish details, such as the stepped facade covered in jewel-like ceramics reminiscent of a medieval tapestry.

**Casa Batlló's ceramic and glass tiles shimmer across the ornate facade. The balconies on the upper floors resemble carnival masks.**

Join the line at **Casa Batlló** *(No. 43, www.casabatllo.es, 934 870 315, €€€€€)* for an audiovisual tour of Gaudí's masterpiece, giving you an insight into his genius. Futuristic construction techniques for cooling systems, or to allow natural light into the inner rooms, became an integral part of the decoration. The glossy blue ceramics in the stairwell subtly grow darker as they near the roof, so the light remains uniform on each floor. Take in all the house's details, from Señor Batlló's office, with its fireplace nook and intricately carved doors, to the catenary arches in the attic, which resemble the rib cage of some mythical creature, and the ergonomic wooden handrail on the stairs. Do not miss the extraordinary roof terrace,

**PASSEIG DE GRÀCIA**

possibly inspired by the tale of Sant Jordi killing the dragon, with the shape of the creature's spine stretching over the house. As you leave take time to appreciate the facade of "the house of bones" with its spindly bone-like balconies and dazzling ceramic tiles formed in the shape of scales.

Passeig de Gràcia between Consell de Cent and Aragó
• Metro: Passeig de Gràcia

## Fundació Antoni Tàpies

**4** See pp. 120–121.

Aragó, 255 • www.fundaciotapies.org • 934 870 315
• €€ • Closed Mon., Jan. 1 and 6, Dec. 25 • Metro:
Passeig de Gràcia

## Rambla de Catalunya

**5** A distinctly different atmosphere prevails on this avenue, stretching from Plaça de Catalunya up to Avinguda Diagonal and cutting through the most sophisticated part of the Eixample. A tree-shaded central boulevard and less traffic give the street a more relaxed pace than parallel Passeig de Gràcia. See the latest exhibition at **Galería Joan Prats** *(No. 54)*, established in 1976 and still part of the art scene. Dip into popular shops like **Zara Home** *(No. 67)*, **Promod** *(No. 80)*, or **Muji** *(No. 81)*. Legendary Catalan designer Toni Miró's original shop **Groc** *(No. 100)* only sells tailored fashion for men. But along the road, his flagship store **Antonio Miró** *(No. 125)* offers his whole range (see pp. 108–109). Pop into classy shopping mall **Bulevard Rosa** *(No. 66)* for some air-conditioned browsing in a wide range of independent boutiques, including stylish handbag maker **Beatriz Furest** or chic children's fashion at **Bóboli.**

Rambla de Catalunya • Metro: Catalunya, Passeig de Gràcia, or Diagonal;
FGC: Provença

## GOOD **EATS**

■ **EL JAPONÉS**
For excellent food in designer surroundings, head to this Japanese restaurant. It serves ceviche, sushi, and their star dish, *kushiyaki* (brochettes). **Passatge de la Concepció, 5, 934 872 592, €€€**

■ **PONSA**
A classic Catalan restaurant in Eixample's prettiest street. Try Catalan dishes such as *espinacs a la catalana* (spinach with raisins and pine nuts) or *fricandó* (beef in a rich sauce). **Enric Granados, 89, 934 531 037, €€**

■ **TAPAS 24**
Squeeze into this basement space to discover the delicate creations of Michelin-starred Carles Abellan, a disciple of Ferran Adrià. He gives a new spin to traditional tapas. **Diputació 269, 934 880 977, €€€**

## La Pedrera (Casa Milà)

**6** Take a seat on one of the white *trencadís* (mosaic) benches situated at intervals along Passeig de Gràcia. Designed by Pere Falqués in 1906, the benches are a good place to absorb the details of Gaudí's Casa Milà, from the sinuous iron and glass main door, past twisted iron balconies, to the "witch-scarer" chimneys protruding above the curved lines of the roof. Try (and fail) to find a straight line in the organic flow of this facade, similar to a rock worn away by the ocean. The impression that the building is hewn from rocks gives it the popular name of La Pedrera, or "quarry." Industrialist Pere Milà i Camps commissioned the apartment building and lived in the *principal,* the spacious first floor.

The official visit takes you onto the roof where the high-profile chimneys and ingenious ventilation shafts stand like sculptures: Enjoy a view of **La Sagrada Família** from this high point. The remarkable attic with its brick catenary arches, similar to those of **Casa Batlló,** holds the **Espai Gaudí,** a permanent exhibition that will help you understand and appreciate the complexity of Gaudí

**La Pedrera's undulating roof with fanciful chimneys offers great views and a venue for concerts.**

and his work. Then see his genius in a typical apartment, **El Pis,** furnished and decorated in early 20th-century style for a bourgeois family. The advanced technical features are astounding, such as the sense of space which comes from having no load-bearing walls. Occasional free exhibitions on the first floor provide an opportunity to see the main staircase and details of the *principal,* useful if you do not have time for a complete visit.

Provença, 261 • www.lapedrera.com • 902 202 138 • €€€€
• Closed Dec. 25 • Metro: Diagonal; FGC: Provença

## IN **THE KNOW**

Don't miss Casa Fuster *(Passeig de Gràcia, 132),* the last building designed by Domènech i Montaner. Built between 1908 and 1911 with lavish materials and a white marble facade, it was said to be the most expensive house in Barcelona. A rich Mallorcan, Mariano Fuster, built the house for his wife. Now a hotel, it holds jazz concerts in its Café Vienés. Stop by to see the sumputous decor reminiscent of the architect's Palau de la Música Catalana (see pp. 96–97).

## Gràcia

**7** Defined by narrow streets with small-scale shops and pretty squares full of terrace cafés, the Gràcia neighborhood has a distinct personality and strong sense of identity. In **Plaça de la Vila de Gràcia,** presided over by the 108-foot (33 m) brick watchtower dating from 1862 and home to the neighborhood's municipal offices, you may come across *castells* or *gegants* during neighborhood fiestas, especially mid-August when the famous *festa major* of Gràcia takes place (see pp. 88–89). Follow the street Mariana Pineda up to the **Plaça del Sol,** Gràcia's unofficial center and a favorite meeting place for people of all ages. Explore the streets off the square to see traditional artisans in workshops alongside stylish fashion boutiques, including El Piano Tina Garcia *(Verdi, 20),* tiny jewelry shops, such as Freya *(Verdi, 17),* and vintage clothes shops. End the day with a cool *canya* (small draught beer) on the terrace of Café del Sol *(Plaça del Sol, 16).* Cinema buffs should head for Cines Verdi *(Verdi, 32),* the best place for movies screened in their original language, known in Spain by the abbreviation V.O.

Metro: Diagonal or Fontana; FGC: Gràcia

# Fundació Antoni Tàpies

*An industrial building of exposed brick and iron complements the contemporary collection of one of Catalonia's most intriguing artists.*

**Tàpies's "Cloud and Chair" rises up from from this old publishing house.**

Antoni Tàpies (1923–2012) remains Spain's best known artist of recent years. A friend and admirer of Miró, his abstract work evolved through many phases, and he used unconventional materials such as concrete. The foundation, set up by the artist himself in 1990, presents a permanent collection of his work alongside a cutting-edge program of temporary modern art exhibitions, showing Tàpies' deep commitment to pluralism and diversity. Begin your visit outside across the street and look up to admire this early *modernista* building.

## ■ THE BUILDING

The artist chose this building carefully, as it celebrates Catalan *modernisme* in humble red bricks and forged metal. It had been built for the publishing house of Montaner i Simon—ideal for an artist inspired by words. Designed by Domènech i Montaner in 1880, the building's elegant lines and Arabic starred motifs soon made it a landmark in Eixample. Now, Tàpies's **"Cloud and Chair"** sculpture seems to float above the foundation, an emblem of artistic contemplation, a key idea for Tàpies. From a tangle of metal wires, a chair rises up into the sky, lifting our eyes and imagination to a higher plane.

## ■ THE WORK

Inside the building, open spaces supported by *modernista* iron columns, where heavy printing presses and offices once stood, provide a perfect setting for Tàpies's work. A selection of art from his large collection changes regularly. Start in the video room on the lower level, where documentaries give an insight into his life and enigmatic work. Tàpies himself was as much alchemist as artist, transforming everyday objects and painting materials into mysterious artworks. **"Metal Shutter and Violin"** on level 1 juxtaposes a silenced musical instrument with a closed, discarded shop shutter; a cross graffittied onto the surface of the work may represent the religious strictures of his early life.

Under Franco's repressive regime, political messages were literally written on walls. Tàpies expressed his own resistance by scratching words and mystic symbols into the surface of his work. For example, liquids poured over the canvas in **"Dyptich in Varnish"** refer to biblical honey as well as bodily functions. Make an appointment to see the **Library,** also on level 1, which houses Tàpies's own book collection on the original shelves of the publishing house.

### IN **THE KNOW**

Take the elevator to the top floor to find a peaceful roof terrace, a typical feature of architecture in Eixample. The work *"Mitjó,"* a large sock sculpture forms a centerpiece. Emblematic of Catalan *seny* and *rauxa* (see p. 72), it shows the transcendent possibilities of art while having its feet literally planted on the ground.

**PASSEIG DE GRÀCIA**

Aragó, 255 • www.fundaciotapies.org • 934 870 315 • €€ • Closed Mon., Jan. 1 and 6, Dec. 25 • Metro: Passeig de Gràcia

# Modernisme

*Modernisme* emerged in Barcelona in the late 19th century at the same time as similar European movements, such as art nouveau. In reaction to classical restraints, *modernista* artists favored flowing forms inspired by the natural world, with floral or animal motifs. In Barcelona, *modernisme* became linked to nationalism, reflecting the city's medieval past in pointed arches and crenellated walls. The movement put a distinct stamp on the city.

The gabled rooftop of Casa Amatller (above) alongside Casa Batlló in the Illa de la Discòrdia. Built by Josep Puig i Cadafalch in 1900 it shows the colorful decoration typical of *modernisme.* The bar in Palau de la Música Catalana (right) also features colored tiles and ceramic molding.

## Architecture

The rise of *modernisme* coincided with the prosperity of the industrial revolution and the construction of the Eixample district. Rich industrialists commissioned enthusiastic young architects with *modernista* ideas to build houses in this new district. The **Quadrat d'Or** (Golden Square), an area around Passeig de Gràcia, showcases the finest architectural examples, from the startling **Illa de la Discòrdia** and **La Pedrera** (see pp. 116–119) to lesser known buildings such as Puig i Cadafalch's neo-Gothic **Palau del Baró de Quadras** (*Diagonal, 373*) or Domènech i Montaner's **Casa Thomas** (*Mallorca, 293*) with its delicate, colored ceramic details and decorative stonework. Visit the basement furniture shop for a closer look at the ornate entrance hall and carvings.

## Decorative Arts

The three leading architects—Antoni Gaudí, Lluís Domènech i Montaner, and Josep Puig i Cadafalch—employed skilled craftsmen to create intricate stonework on facades and staircases; ceramic creations on wall coverings and chimney pots; and wrought iron and glass in windows, doors, and lamps. Domènech i Montaner's **Palau de la Música Catalana** (see pp. 96–97) shows a range of decorative finishes in one building. Walk around the Eixample and peep into doorways to see the rich designs and stained-glass covered balconies.

Gaudí also designed furniture, as seen in the **Casa Batlló** (see pp. 116–117), following natural, organic forms, a fundamental theme in *modernisme*. See the furnishings, paintings, and sculpture that may have decorated these buildings in the **Museu del Modernisme Català** (see p. 143), located in a *modernista* house designed by Enric Sagnier.

## MODERNISTA BUILDINGS

Lesser known examples are:

**Antigua Casa Figueras** An ornate Escribà chocolate shop. **La Rambla, 83**

**Casa Vicens** An early Gaudí house with bright tiles. **Carolines, 24**

**Central Catalana d'Electricitat** Industrial architecture. **Vilanova, 12**

**Els Quatre Gats bar** A meeting place for bohemian artists. **Montsió, 3**

**Hospital de la Santa Creu i Sant Pau** A former hospital (see pp. 130–131). **Sant Antoni Maria Claret, 167**

# Coffee & Cava

Bars in Barcelona range from cafés serving snacks to sophisticated cocktail bars. They are places to have your first cup of coffee, prelunch *vermut,* evening *cava* and tapas, and *última copa* (last drink before going home). These bars are arranged according to what you might want at different times of the day.

■ OFF TO A GOOD START

Most people breakfast in a bar on their way to work or leave the office mid-morning for a strong *solo.* Join them in the Passeig de Gràcia area at **Café Zurich** (see p. 114), one of the most famous cafés in the city. Or try a **Bracafé,** which has branches across town. The best one, near Passeig de Gràcia *(Casp, 2),* serves full-flavor Brazilian coffee from 6:30 a.m. Popular with traders at the nearby stock exchange, it opened for the 1929 Exhibition. Hidden at the rear of the dynamic CCCB (see p. 65) in El Raval, **C3Bar's** *(Montalegre, 5)* terrace catches the sun. In the atmospheric **Cafè de l'Òpera** *(La Rambla, 74)* you can read quietly in the morning at a marble table. The atmosphere builds to a noisy crescendo in early evening, when operagoers on La Rambla drop in for a drink before the curtain call.

■ ALL–DAY LONG

One of the most authentic local bars in Gràcia (see p. 119), **Roure** *(Luis Antúnez, 7),* with efficient waiters in crisp white shirts, looks almost the same as when it opened in 1889. In La Rambla, enjoy a cool beer any time of day in traditional bars, such as **Castells** *(Plaça Bonsuccés, 1).* Jostle with the regulars at the sturdy marble bar and request a plate of *pernil ibèric* (Iberian ham) or *truita* (Spanish omelette made with spinach, potato, or eggplant). In Barri Gòtic, family run **Bar del Pi** *(Plaça Sant Josep Oriol, 1)* has a handsome bar and timeless atmosphere, though most people prefer a table outside in the picturesque square (see p. 49). For a pick-me-up when sightseeing in La Ribera, drop into petite, fully tiled **El Xampanyet** (see p. 30) near Museu Picasso, where they have been serving *cava* since 1929.

El Xampanyet serves *cava* as well as coffee, beer, and tapas throughout the day.

### ■ COCKTAIL HOUR & BEYOND

A short walk from Passeig de Gràcia, **Dry Martini** *(Aribau, 162)* ranks in the top 50 bars in the world year after year. Leather banquettes, a wooden bar with brass trimmings, white-jacketed waiters, and dry martinis that would please Dorothy Parker give it all the essential ingredients of a cocktail bar. In the center of the Eixample neighborhood, not far from Passeig de Gràcia, discover **Hotel Alma** *(Mallorca, 271)*. On warm evenings, the lush interior garden makes a perfect setting for a drink. **Ginger** *(Lledó, 2)*, in the heart of Barri Gòtic, has the intimacy and comfort of a private club—complement your drink with a selection of tapas. On the waterfront taste the high life at **Eclipse** on the 26th floor of the W hotel *(Plaça de la Rosa dels Vents, 1, 932 952 800)*. Mingle with the jet set and gaze at one of the best views in town until 4 a.m. on weekends and 2 a.m. Monday to Thursday; it gets packed after 11 p.m., so make a reservation. Near Montjuïc, go to the Poble Sec area for a gin and tonic at **Xixbar** *(Rocafort, 19)*. The pretty surroundings of a converted 19th–century dairy, create a small and chic bar space.

# La Sagrada Família to Park Güell

Contemporary architecture contrasts with *modernista* masterworks in this section of Eixample. Jean Nouvel's towering Torre Agbar represents modern Barcelona, while Gaudí's famous park and church have become the city's icons. The spires of La Sagrada Família, Gaudí's great unfinished work, rise up over an area undergoing renewal, just as the epic project nears completion. A new cultural center will emerge in the *modernista* complex of the Hospital San Pau, designed by Lluís Domènech i Montaner. Plaça de les Glòries forms the gateway to 22@, a new high-tech business district. In addition to the shimmering Torre Agbar, the DHUB design museum is set to become another modern landmark. In the north of the neighborhood, Gaudí's dreamlike Park Güell still captures the imagination of visitors.

◀ **La Sagrada Família will have twelve towers for the Apostles, four more for the Evangelists, one for the Virgin Mary, and a central tower for Christ when finished.**

# La Sagrada Família to Park Güell

*Architectural wonders from the 19th, 20th, and 21st centuries abound in the matrix of streets around La Sagrada Família.*

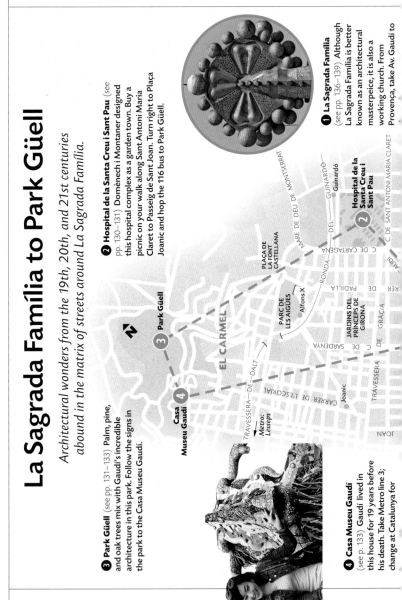

**2 Hospital de la Santa Creu i Sant Pau** (see pp. 130–131) Domènech i Montaner designed this hospital complex as a garden town. Buy a picnic on your walk along Sant Antoni Maria Claret to Passeig de Sant Joan. Turn right to Plaça Joanic and hop the 116 bus to Park Güell.

**1 La Sagrada Família** (see pp. 136–139) Although La Sagrada Família is better known as an architectural masterpiece, it is also a working church. From Provença, take Av. Gaudí to

**3 Park Güell** (see pp. 131–133) Palm, pine, and oak trees mix with Gaudí's incredible architecture in this park. Follow the signs in the park to the Casa Museu Gaudí.

**4 Casa Museu Gaudí** (see p. 133) Gaudí lived in this house for 19 years before his death. Take Metro line 3; change at Catalunya for

**Plaça de les Glòries**
(see p. 135) The Torre Agbar has 4,500 windows to light the interior by day. Walk around the plaza as it becomes dark to watch the tower light up.

**6 DHUB** (see p. 134) The brutalist form of the new design museum makes a statement. Around the periphery, a green zone and artificial lake soften the space.

**5 L'Auditori & Museu de la Música** (see p. 134) Housed in a modern building, this concert hall and museum are part of the new highbrow cultural hub of Barcelona. Turn left onto Ali Bei and left again onto Meridiana.

**LA SAGRADA FAMÍLIA TO PARK GÜELL. DISTANCE: APPROX 5 MILES (8 KM)**
**TIME: APPROX. 9 HOURS METRO START: SAGRADA FAMÍLIA**

## La Sagrada Família

**1** See pp. 136–139.

Mallorca, 401 • www.sagradafamilia.org • 935 132 060 • €€€ (without audioguide or access to towers) • Metro: Sagrada Família

## Hospital de la Santa Creu i Sant Pau

**2** Take a guided tour around the Hospital de la Santa Creu i Sant Pau to visit some of the buildings or wander through the streets and explore the gardens at your own pace. This complex may be one of the most underrated *modernista* sites in Barcelona—it was a hospital and could not be seen easily by the casual visitor until recently. In 2009, the medical facilities were moved to a modern complex on the same gargantuan block—leaving conservationists

A combination of red bricks and colorful ceramics cover the hospital's domes and turrets.

and historians the formidable task of restoring the old hospital's abundant artistic and architectural glory.

Lluís Domènech i Montaner designed the Hospital de la Santa Creu i Sant Pau as a community for those suffering from plagues and contagious diseases. His concept was for a group of individual redbrick pavilion-wards, connected by a network of underground tunnels to enable staff to move patients around easily. Domènech i Montaner believed in the therapeutic value of light and beautiful surroundings. If you take the tour, you will notice each building has a different design, with florid ceramics, sculpture, mosaics, and stained glass. As you walk along the small streets between the buildings, notice rose and herb gardens: These are designed to create the feeling of a small town. Visit the church that the locals still use; inside, two lions guard alabaster staircases to a pair of pulpits. The hospital complex took such a long time to build, from 1901 to 1930, that the architect's son had to complete the work.

Research and cultural associations will move into the old hospital pavilions as each one is completed. The whole work is scheduled to finish by 2017.

Sant Antoni María Claret, 167 • www.barcelonaturisme.com/L-Hospital-de-la-Santa-Creu-i-Sant-Pau • 933 177 652 • Closed Jan. 1 and 6, Dec. 25–26 • Guided tours in English daily at 10 a.m., 11 a.m., noon, and 1 p.m. • Metro: Hospital de Sant Pau

## Park Güell

**3** Either walk up the steep hill or hop a bus to the upper slopes of Barcelona to enjoy Gaudí's most accessible and crowd-pleasing gift to the city—Park Güell. In 1902, Eusebi Güell commissioned Gaudí to create a garden estate, where wealthy clients could purchase land and build houses with stunning views. The residents would enjoy amenities such as a marketplace,

### SAVVY **TRAVELER**

The authorities recently became concerned that the large number of visitors to Park Güell may damage its artworks and vegetation. An entry fee has been introduced (you will need another ticket for the Casa Museu Gaudí), and tourists will be limited to 800 in the most popular areas. The park can seem crowded, but the area at the top, near the chapel, is usually quiet.

The Sala Hipóstila at Park Güell towers over the main staircase, offering great views from the roof.

plaza, and chapel, all designed by the great architect. But the venture failed to attract investors, and eventually the city acquired the land for a public park (see p. 140).

Gaudí's vivid imagination created an atmospheric series of terraces and buildings across the park. As you arrive, the main entrance evokes the sensation of stepping into a fairy tale. On either side of the gateway sit two brightly colored pavilions, possibly inspired by the legend of Hansel and Gretel and originally intended as gatehouses. Ascend a grand staircase leading to the first plateau, guarded by the park's famous, and much photographed, dragon and fountain. Notice the *trencadís,* broken pieces of glass and china that cover the surfaces and became one of Gaudí's signature features. At the top of the stairs, the **Sala Hipóstila,** planned to be the estate's covered market, forms a majestic hall supported by more than 80 Doric columns, some leaning inward. The undulating roof supports another of the park's star attractions, a serpentine bench that winds around the edge and is the perfect spot for lunch with a view.

Olot, 5 • €€ • Metro: Lesseps; Bus: 24 , 31, 32

## Casa Museu Gaudí

**4** Inside Park Güell, visit a pretty pink *torre* (freestanding house) designed by friend and associate, Francesc Berenguer i Mestres. Gaudí made his home here from 1906 until 1925, a few months before his death. Gaudí bought the *torre rosa*, originally the show home for the proposed development in the park(see pp. 131–132), and moved in with his father and niece after it became clear that the other 60 houses would not be built.

Look at the outside of the three-story home and compare its pointed tower and straight lines with Gaudí's curving, extravagant designs elsewhere in the park. As you enter the house notice the heavy dark wood decor and floors of colored tiles, typical of the formal taste of the time. You will see examples of the furniture that Gaudí designed for **Casa Calvet** and **Casa Batlló** (see pp. 116–117), as well as the inspirational plans and drawings for their fluid shapes. End your visit upstairs, where his bedroom has been reconstructed, with a prayer book on a table next to his plain bed. This simple room reflects Gaudí's austere, religious personal taste. Gaudí's death mask, also on display, completes a reverent homage to the great architect.

Carmel • www.casamuseugaudi.org • 932 193 811 • €€ • Metro: Lesseps; Bus: 24, 31, 32

**The simple lines of Gaudí's home contrast with his extravagant designs for Park Güell.**

## GOOD **EATS**

### ■ ALKIMIA
For haute cuisine, reserve a table at the Michelin-starred Alkimia restaurant. Succumb to the inventive dishes of the chef, Jordi Vila, who offers seasonal menus and a good-value lunch option. **Indústria, 79, 932 076 115, €€€€€**

### ■ CAN RAVELL
Head to the tiny dining room of this traditional deli and wine shop for one of the best food experiences in Barcelona. Established in 1929, Can Ravell serves immaculately prepared traditional Catalan fare. **Aragó, 313, 934 575 114, €€€€**

### ■ LU LU TONG
A "Chinatown" district has mushroomed around the Plaça Tetuan, offering cheap and tasty meals in no-nonsense settings. Try Lu Lu Tong for homemade noodle dishes and wanton soup. **Diputació, 340, 932 656 178, €**

## L'Auditori & Museu de la Música

**5** Spend the afternoon and evening in the new cultural district south of La Sagrada Família. L'Auditori opened in 1994 as a modern alternative to the Palau de la Música Catalana (see pp. 96–97). This accoustically faultless music hall hosts top musicians; try to return later for a performance. Admire the work of Rafael Moneo, one of Spain's most prestigious and elegant architects. The building's strong lines were inspired by the grid pattern of the surrounding Eixample district.

Inside the building, visit the Museu de la Música, situated on the second floor around a central skylight that illuminates the space. The museum displays about 500 instruments from a collection of more than 1,600 pieces dating from the 17th century. In addition, musical gadgets, pianola rolls, and other automated inventions complete the exhibit.

Lepant, 150 • www.bcn.cat/museumusica • 932 563 650 • Closed Tues., Jan. 1, Good Friday, May 1, June 24, Dec. 25–26 • € • Metro: Glòries

## DHUB

**6** The new DHUB, Design Hub Barcelona, celebrates the city's rich design culture in a museum that brings together four collections of art and design, previously scattered across the city in smaller displays. The exhibition spans everything from 16th-century ceramics to haute couture fashion, and advertising posters to industrial design. Displayed in a building designed by local studio MBM, and making use of a natural slope, part of the structure extends underground with a large lake outside. Check the DHUB website for events and architectural tours of Barcelona.

Plaça de les Glòries, 37–38 • www.dhub-bcn.cat • 932 566 713 • Metro: Glòries

## Plaça de les Glòries

**7** For decades the main attraction in the Plaça de les Glòries was **Els Encants** market (see p. 108), but now even this famous flea market has smarter premises in the revitalized area. Ildefons Cerdà, the original designer of the Eixample district, wanted to create a huge square, but it did not happen, and the "plaza" was a traffic circle until French architect Jean Nouvel's **Torre Agbar** put the area on the map in 2005. Accommodating the HQ of the local water authority, this 466-foot-high (142 m) beacon lights the night sky with a shimmering "skin" of colored LED lights. It acts as a gateway to **22@,** the city's high-tech business district, where you can see some of the latest innovative architecture . Seek out Enric Ruiz Geli's futuristic, energy efficient **Media-TIC** building and the **Can Framis** museum (see p. 142).

Av. Diagonal, Gran Via de les Corts Catalanes, and Av. Meridiana • Metro: Glòries

**The 31-story Torre Agbar dominates the night sky with 4,500 colored lights.**

# La Sagrada Família

*You will need two hours to take in all the details on the building, from the brilliantly colored mosaics to the intricate carvings.*

The splendor of La Sagrada Família begins to emerge from the scaffolding after more than a century.

Antoni Gaudí's La Sagrada Família, one of the most visited monuments in the world, has become an unofficial emblem of Barcelona despite still being a work in progress. The neo-Gothic church started by Villar in 1882 began to change radically when 31-year-old Gaudí took charge a year later. This monumental church became the central project for the devout Gaudí, who moved into the workshop shortly before his death in 1926. He is buried in the crypt of this unique church, later consecrated as a basilica by Pope Benedict XVI in 2010.

## ■ URBAN SURROUNDINGS

You need to see the building from several blocks away to get the full impact of its scale. The eight towers reach for the sky from behind the surrounding buildings, and huge cranes mingle with them as if part of the design. Buy tickets, either online or at the site, and pay for an audio guide, or follow the information boards inside.

## ■ PASSION FACADE

Begin your visit at the **Passion facade,** built according to the original plans, but with sculptures added by Catalan artist Josep Maria Subirachs since 1986. They have been criticized for not fitting in with the church's organic style, although Gaudí expected future generations to make their own imprint. The figures have sharp angular lines, accentuating the Passion, the harsh story of the crucifixion, amid the bone-like porticoes. Notice the symbolic details, such as the cryptogram by the statue of **Judas' Kiss** where combinations of numbers add up to 33, the age Christ died. Find Gaudí's face among the statues, a tribute to the maestro from Subirachs. Peer up to see the bronze sculpture representing the **Ascension** which hovers over the door—it is

### IN **THE KNOW**

Gaudí died in 1926 as he walked from his workshop in La Sagrada Família to Sant Felip Neri church (see p. 50) in the Barri Gòtic district. He was hit by a tram as he crossed Gran Via. At first, people mistook Gaudí for a pauper because he was wearing old work clothes. He was taken to the Antic Hospital de la Sant Creu (see p. 66), where he died a few days later. Barcelona gave Gaudí a hero's funeral.

16.4 feet (5 m) long and weighs more than 4,000 pounds (1,814 kg). Go up the steps and observe the complex detail on the bronze doors, also by Subirachs, embedded with gadgets, from screws and coins to words from the Bible in Catalan.

## ■ THE INTERIOR

Pass through the heavy doors into a vast space where up to 8,000 people and 1,200 choristers can worship. A huge step forward came 84 years after Gaudí's death when the nave was covered and consecrated for worship by the pope. Dappled light filters through skylights in the ceiling and stained-glass windows designed by Joan Vila-Grau. In this space that is half building site and half sacred place, you may hear an organ playing, the celestial sound punctuated with drilling from on high. Don't be surprised to see a wheelbarrow suspended in midair on its way up to one of the 18 towers that will eventually crown the church. Elegant columns twist and turn, branching off toward the top to create the forest effect Gaudí intended. The complex geometry behind their design follows Gaudí's observation of nature, a constant in his work. Likewise, the light features in the columns resemble knots in trees. As you approach the altar, look up at the glorious skylight above, a hyperboloid form lined with golden tiles that glow to represent God. Walk around the back of the altar to

## SAVVY **TRAVELLER**

Skip the notorious lines for tickets by buying online (http://visit .sagradafamilia.cat). Choose the time you wish to visit and walk straight in. Buy tickets to the towers at the same time. Avoid weekends and Mondays, a favorite as most museums are closed. If you opt for a time slot at the end of the day, you may dodge the group tours. Allow two hours for your visit.

see the chapels, including one with a confessional designed by Gaudí.

### ■ NATIVITY FACADE

Leave through the east door and stand back to check out all the details on this facade, the only one Gaudí lived to see completed. Dripping with stone, evidently inspired by geological phenomena found in Catalonia, the sculptures tell the story of the Nativity and depict events from the life of Christ. A green ceramic cypress tree crowns the scenes. From here go into the **Rosario cloister,** dedicated to our Lady of the Rosary. The cloister will eventually run around the whole church. Among the sculptures, look for the anarchist with his bomb, embodying the evil of mankind.

**Subirachs' portrait of Pontius Pilate can be found on the Passion facade.**

### ■ GREAT VIEWS

In the cloister area, you can catch an elevator to visit the two bell towers. Ride to the top for a panoramic view across Barcelona. The ride also gives you an opportunity to see the carvings on the **Nativity facade** close-up. Do not miss the Venetian glass *trencadís* (mosaics) that top the highest pinnacles of the church.

### ■ MUSEUM & SCHOOL

Allow time to visit the informative museum at the end of the tour. It contains fascinating photographs of the early days of construction, architectural models, and illuminating explanations of Gaudí's vision for the church.

The museum leads you back to the Passion facade where you can find the **Edifici de les Escoles,** the school Gaudí built for the local children and those of people working on the church. Its simple but ingenious format with a curved roof and walls is said to have impressed another great 20th-century architect, Le Corbusier.

### ■ END IN SIGHT

Like many other grand cathedrals, the construction work on the building

**The stone carving on the Nativity facade is full of intricate details.**

has already spanned more than a hundred years and it will continue well into the 21st century. Successive generations continue to build in the spirit of Gaudí's vision, although today they are aided by the latest computer technology.

The **Torre de Jesucrist,** the tallest tower, should reach its full height of 566 feet (173 m) by 2020. The final completion date forecast for La Sagrada Família is 2026, one hundred years after Gaudí's death.

Mallorca, 401 • www.sagradafamilia.org • 935 132 060 • €€€ (without audioguide or access to towers) • Metro: Sagrada Família

# Parks & Gardens

The dense, historic streets that make the old town such a great place to explore left little room for parks or gardens. A palm tree in an inner courtyard was as good as it got. However, the city's expansion in the 19th century and development of neglected land for grand events provided open areas that gradually became part of the urban landscape. The revolutionary urban renewal program that began in the 1980s created many modern parks.

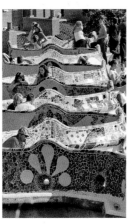

**Crowds enjoy the serpentine bench (above) at Park Güell, designed by Josep Maria Jujol, who worked with Gaudí on the project. An earlier example of Gaudí's work can be seen in the Cascada (right), which he helped to design for Parc de la Ciutadella.**

### Accidental Gardens

Some of Barcelona's most distinctive parks developed through quirks of history and expansion. The failure of Eusebi Güell's project gave the town land for its citizens to enjoy in 1923. Luckily Gaudí, the estate's architect, had already landscaped the hillside, so **Park Güell** (see pp. 131–133) bears his inimitable stamp, with fluid walkways and colorful ceramics. The city's oldest public park, **Parc de la Ciutadella** (see pp. 34, 100–101), also began in another guise, as the 1888 International Exhibition site. You can still enjoy the cultural legacy of *modernista* buildings, such as the **Castell dels Tres Dragons** and the iron and glass **Hivernacle.**

The 1929 International Exhibition led to the landscaping of Montjuïc, creating formal gardens, such as the **Jardins del Teatre Grec**, with cypress hedges and wisteria-clad pergolas. They make a stunning backdrop to an evening performance in the amphitheater during the summer Grec Festival. The **Jardins de Laribal** take inspiration from the gardens of southern Spain, with shady terraces, balustrades, and small lily-covered ponds.

## New Urban Spaces

Barcelona's new parks emerged in the 1980s on obsolete industrial land or areas of demolished housing. The first of these, **Parc de Joan Miró** (see p. 59), built over a former slaughterhouse, combines elements of these new spaces: trees, mixed vegetation, ponds, play areas, and works of art. Beverly Pepper's blue ceramic sculpture **"Cel caigut"** ("Fallen sky") graces **Parc de l'Estació del Nord,** the site of an old station. A futuristic park of lawns and concrete near Sants station, **Parc de l'Espanya Industrial,** occupies the land of a former textile factory—rent a boat to cross its lake.

## CITY **COURTYARDS**

Town planner Ildefons Cerdà's 1859 utopian scheme for Eixample featured U-shaped blocks with an inner green space. But the plans were adapted, resulting in the four-sided blocks of the neighborhood. Recently, some inner patios have been recovered to create public gardens with benches and games for kids. On your way to La Sagrada Família check out **Jardins del Rector Oliveras** (Aragó, 309), **Jardins de Jaume Perich** (Gran Via, 657), or the "Eixample beach" in **La Torre de les Aigües** (see p. 59).

# Small Museums

Barcelona has a host of fascinating small museums, many gathered from private collections or singular obsessions. Can Framis, near La Sagrada Família, exhibits work from the collection of Antoni Vila Casas. Other museums show priceless Egyptian antiquities, contemporary art, or musical instruments.

### ■ CAN FRAMIS

Near La Sagrada Família, this award-winning conversion of a 19th-century textile factory forms part of the Plaça de les Glòries cultural area. It displays Catalan art from the 1970s onward. A smaller gallery hosts shows of art on loan from private collectors.

Roc Boronat, 116–126 • www.fundaciovilacasas .com • 933 208 736 • € • Closed Mon., Sun. p.m., public holidays, summer, Dec. 24–Jan. 1 • Metro: Glòries

### ■ MUSEU DEL CALÇAT

In Barri Gòtic, this quirky museum is housed in the Gothic hall of the shoemaker's guild—the city's oldest (see p. 50). It's an evocative space, where you can see reproductions of shoes from the 18th century onward, as well as tools of this ancient trade.

Plaça de Sant Felip Neri, 5 • 933 014 533 • € • 11 a.m.– 2p.m., closed Mon. • Metro: Jaume I

### ■ MUSEU DE LA XOCOLATA

In La Ribera, this museum (see p. 35), established by the city's pastry making guild, traces chocolate's journey from the Americas to Europe—an event Catalans have taken credit for.

Comerç, 36 • www.museuxocolata.cat • 932 687 878 • € • Closed Sun. and public holidays p.m. • Metro: Jaume I or Arc de Triomf

### ■ FUNDACIÓ FRANCISCO GODIA

In a *modernista* house near Passeig de Gràcia, this museum showcases medieval paintings and ceramics collected by Formula One driver Francisco Godia (1921–1990). After his death, his daughter set up the foundation to display the 1,500 works, from Catalan Gothic to modern artists, including Antoni Tàpies.

Diputació, 250 • www.fundacionfgodia.org • 932 723 180 • €€ • Closed Tues., Sun. p.m., and public holidays • Metro: Passeig de Grácia

**A chocolate king and queen await visitors to the chocolate museum.**

### ■ FUNDACIÓ SUÑOL

Head to this gallery near Passeig de Gràcia to see a collection of contemporary art including Picasso and Susana Solano. A separate space, Nivell Zero, hosts temporary shows from new artists.

Passeig de Gràcia, 98 • www.fundaciosunol.org • 934 961 032 • €€ • Closed Sat. a.m., Sun., and public holidays • Metro: Diagonal

### ■ MUSEU EGIPCI DE BARCELONA

In a road off Passeig de Gràcia, discover mummies and more in a museum set up by the hotelier and collector of ancient Egyptian artifacts, Jordi Clos.

València, 284 • www.museuegipci.com • 934 880 188 • €€€ • Closed Sun. p.m., Jan. 1 and 6, Dec. 25–26 • Metro: Passeig de Gràcia

### ■ MUSEU DEL MODERNISME CATALÀ

While in Passeig de Gràcia, marvel at Barcelona's *modernista* architecture (see pp. 122–123), then visit this museum, on a parallel road, to see furniture, paintings, and decorative arts. Standout pieces include Gaudí's furniture and the paintings of Ramón Casas and Santiago Rusiñol that evoke the grace of the period.

Balmes, 48 • www.mmcat.cat • 932 722 896 • €€ • Closed Sun. p.m., Jan. 1 and 6, May 1, Dec. 25–26 • Metro: Passeig de Gràcia

# Camp Nou to Tibidabo

South of Diagonal Avenue the lively Camp Nou (New Field) soccer stadium contrasts with the tranquil Barrios Altos (uptown neighborhoods) to the north. Once a string of outlying villages, but now a part of the city, leafy Pedralbes and Sarrià feature stately mansions, *torres,* many built in the *modernista* style. These houses sit cheek by jowl with posh boutiques, fashionable restaurants, and exclusive apartment buildings. Head to the monastery in Pedralbes, then enjoy the gourmet delis and village ambiance of Sarrià. *Jabalíes* (wild boar) have been known to wander down from Tibidabo, one of Barcelona's twin peaks—maybe searching for scraps from Sarrià's tapas bars. Take the city's oldest tram to the Parc d'Atraccions del Tibidabo, an amusement park next to a huge church, for a great view of Barcelona.

◖ **A colorful Ferris wheel, the "Panoramic" has tempted visitors to Tibidabo for decades.**

# Camp Nou to Tibidabo

*An uphill walk takes in sports and science museums, tranquil gardens, and a monastery, and ends with exciting rides at the top of a hill.*

**4 Sarrià** (see p. 149) Visit upscale Sarrià to see Sant Vincenç church and a lively market built in the *modernista* style. Stop for lunch or a snack in one of the many restaurants and cafés. Then continue along Passeig Reina Elisenda de Montcada to Plaça John F. Kennedy, or hop the 58 or 75 bus.

**3 Monestir de Pedralbes** (see pp. 152–153) This monastic complex has remained remarkably intact since its foundation in 1326. It contains an enchanting cloister and valuable Renaissance art. Walk back to Bisbe Català and continue until you reach Plaça Sarrià.

**2 Parc and Palau Reial de Pedralbes** (see pp. 148–149) Stroll through the formal gardens of this elegant mansion, then walk up Av. de Pedralbes past some of the most exclusive apartments in town. Turn right at the top onto Bisbe Català, and left into the Baixada del Monestir.

**1 Museu del FC Barcelona** (see p. 148) Step inside Camp Nou (New Field) stadium to visit the FC Barcelona Museum celebrating Barça, arguably the most famous soccer club in the world. Walk along Arístides Maillol to the end, turn right, then left onto Marti i Franqués, and continue to Diagonal.

PLAÇA DEL MONESTIR
Monestir de Pedralbes
3
AVINGUDA DE PEDRALBES
PEDRALBES
Parc and Palau Reial de Pedralbes
2
AVINGUDA DIAGONAL
PARC DE PEDRALBES
Palau Reial
ZONA UNIVERSITÀRIA
PLAÇA DE PIUS XII
Maria Cristina
PLAÇA DE LA REINA MARIA CRISTINA
AVINGUDA DIAG
GRAN VIA DE CARLES III
Museu del FC Barcelona
1
TRAVESSERA DE LES CORTS
LES CORTS
Les Corts
TRAVESSERA DE LES
AVINGUDA DE MADRID

**CAMP NOU TO TIBIDABO DISTANCE: 3.7 MILES (6 KM)**
**TIME: APPROX. 8 HOURS METRO START: LES CORTS**

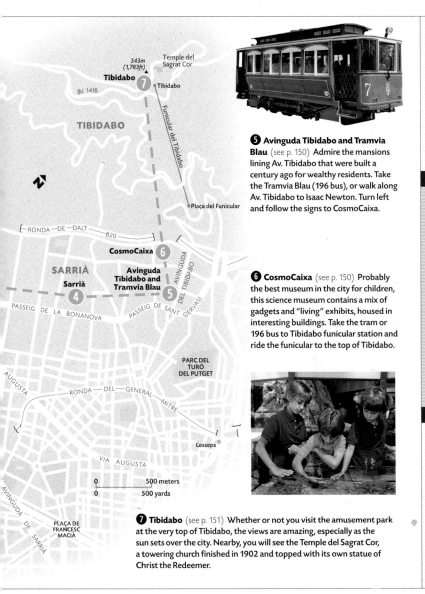

543m
(1,783ft)
**Tibidabo**  ⑦  • Tibidabo

BV 1418

Temple del
Sagrat Cor

**TIBIDABO**

Funicular del Tibidabo

• Plaça del Funicular

RONDA — DE — DALT    B20

**CosmoCaixa**  ⑥

**SARRIÀ**     **Avinguda**
            **Tibidabo and**
**Sarrià**  ④  **Tramvia Blau**  ⑤

AVINGUDA DEL TIBIDABO

PASSEIG DE LA BONANOVA

PASSEIG DE SANT GERVASI

PARC DEL
TURÓ
DEL PUTGET

AUGUSTA

RONDA — DEL — GENERAL — MITRE

• Lesseps

VIA  AUGUSTA

0 _____ 500 meters
0 _____ 500 yards

AVINGUDA DE SARRIÀ

PLAÇA DE
FRANCESC
MACIÀ

**⑤ Avinguda Tibidabo and Tramvia
Blau** (see p. 150)  Admire the mansions
lining Av. Tibidabo that were built a
century ago for wealthy residents. Take
the Tramvia Blau (196 bus), or walk along
Av. Tibidabo to Isaac Newton. Turn left
and follow the signs to CosmoCaixa.

**⑥ CosmoCaixa** (see p. 150)  Probably
the best museum in the city for children,
this science museum contains a mix of
gadgets and "living" exhibits, housed in
interesting buildings. Take the tram or
196 bus to Tibidabo funicular station and
ride the funicular to the top of Tibidabo.

**⑦ Tibidabo** (see p. 151)  Whether or not you visit the amusement park
at the very top of Tibidabo, the views are amazing, especially as the
sun sets over the city. Nearby, you will see the Temple del Sagrat Cor,
a towering church finished in 1902 and topped with its own statue of
Christ the Redeemer.

### Museu del FC Barcelona

**1** Camp Nou soccer stadium (see pp. 154–155, 173), the largest in Europe, houses the FC Barcelona Museum on its ground floor. Once inside, immerse yourself in the club's history and achievements through photographs, interactive displays, trophies, and other memorabilia. Soccer fans should pay the extra fee for the stadium tour in the **"Camp Nou Experience."** Avoid waiting in line at this popular museum by buying tickets in advance.

Calle Aristides Maillol, 12 • www.fcbarcelona.com • 902 189 900 • €€€€€ • Closed Jan. 1 and 6, Dec. 25 • Metro: Les Corts

### Parc and Palau Reial de Pedralbes

**2** Head off bustling Diagonal Avenue and spend some time exploring this stately park filled with bougainvillea and cedars. The park once formed the grounds of the Royal Palace of Pedralbes.

The Royal Palace of Pedralbes became a retreat for King Alfonso XIII in the 1920s.

Now awaiting redevelopment, the palace has been home to Gaudí's main client, industrialist Eusebi Güell, a royal retreat, headquarters of the Republican goverment, Franco's weekend pad, and a museum. Walk beneath shady trees beside ponds and flower beds in this tranquil park. A summer music festival attracts international artists, including Natalie Cole and Anthony and the Johnsons.

### SAVVY **TRAVELER**

Metro stops in the Barrios Altos are few and far between, so use the buses and the tram. Also, try the FGC—a rail network that extends to the area (see p. 177).

As you leave the park, turn onto Avinguda de Pedralbes and stop to admire the **Pavellons de la Finca Güell.** You will see a stunning gate, and through that glimpse a gatehouse and a stable, all designed by Gaudí for Eusebi Güell's estate, which later became the Palau Reial de Pedralbes. The gate twists and curves in the shape of a fiery dragon wrought into a frightening pose with masterful ironwork. The two curious pavilions once housed the caretaker and horses. Built in an exotic eastern style, the buildings feature corbel roofs and *trencadís* facades of colorful ceramic mosaic.

Diagonal, 686 • Metro: Palau Reial

## Monestir de Pedralbes

**3** See pp. 152–153.

Baixada de Monestir, 9 • www.museuhistoria.bcn.es • 932 563 434 • €€ • Closed Mon., Jan. 1, May 1, June 24, Dec. 25 • FGC: Reina Elisenda

## Sarrià

**4** Sarrià dwellers claim that the air is cleaner in their hillside homes, and on a humid day it's hard to argue. Sarrià was the last independent town to be annexed into Barcelona, and it still has its own distinct feel. Head to Major de Sarrià for posh gourmet shops and boutiques. Stop for coffee and cake at **Foix de Sarrià** (see p. 150), a famous pastry and candy shop with two branches in the area.

Sarrià • FGC: Sarrià

## GOOD **EATS**

■ **BAR TOMÁS**
Try the best *patatas bravas* in town at this local bar. The special sauce topping the fried potatoes makes them famous. **Major de Sarrià, 49, 932 031 077, €**

■ **FOIX DE SARRIÀ**
Since 1886, this bakery has been dishing up buttery croissants, elaborate cakes, Catalan *cocas* (sweet bread), chocolates, and savory deli delights from their *modernista* premises. There are two branches, the original is: **Major de Sarrià, 57, 932 030 714, €**

■ **FRAGMENTS CAFÉ**
This old-style tapas bar and restaurant has a handful of tables on Plaça de la Concòrdia and in a lovely rear garden. Dishes are market fresh—try the excellent value lunch menu. **Plaça de la Concòrdia, 12, 934 199 613, €€**

## Avinguda Tibidabo & Tramvia Blau

**5** The quaint Tramvia Blau (Blue Tram) has been rattling up swanky Avinguda de Tibidabo since 1901. Before you get on, stop to admire the beautiful *modernista* landmark, **La Rotonda,** covered with colorful mosaics. Hop aboard the tram for a short ride past elegant fin de siécle villas as it wends its way to Tibidabo funicular station. Along the way, look out for the tall, distinctive **Casa Roviralta** at No. 31. Now a restaurant, this Mudéjar-inspired building has a white and brick exterior, and you can see some of the rooms inside if you return for dinner.

Av. Tibidabo • www.tmb.cat • FGC: Av. Tibidabo

## CosmoCaixa

**6** In 2005, a dramatic modern building joined to a handsome *modernista* hospital dating from 1894 became Barcelona's science museum. Visitors are greeted by a statue of Albert Einstein before descending down a huge spiral staircase with a tropical tree growing in the central space. Once in the basement, learn about geographic and scientific principles with special experiments and equipment. A wave simulator shows how the sea forms the shores, and you can create a sandstorm or a tornado. The **Flooded Forest** gives an idea of life in an Amazon forest with real plants and a few animals—some roam freely, but the crocodiles and snakes are kept behind barriers. Rain showers water the area regularly and add to the atmosphere. Gaze at the stars and planets in the **Planetarium** before trying more experiments in the vast area outside the museum. One display demonstrates sound wave transmission between two satellite dishes.

Isaac Newton, 26 • www.fundacio.lacaixa.es • 932 126 050 • € • Closed Mon. except public holidays, Jan. 1 and 6, Dec. 25 • FGC: Av. Tibidabo and Tramvia Blau; Bus: 196

## Tibidabo

**7** At nearly 2,000 feet (610 m) high, the Tibidabo summit to Barcelona's northwest affords great views of the city. Ride the elevator to the top of the church, **Temple del Sagrat Cor,** for an even higher viewpoint. The highlight, though, is the **Parc d'Atraccions,** the oldest amusement park in Spain. Opened in 1901, it now has some high-tech rides, though a few low-tech ones remain. Outside the main park, the **Camí de Cel,** or Sky Walk, has more gentle rides for small children; it includes one of the park's most emblamatic rides representing the first plane to fly the Barcelona–Madrid route.

Tibidabo • www.tibidabo.cat • 932 117 942• €€€€€ • Check website for opening times • FGC: Av. Tibidabo (then Tramvia Blau or 196 bus to Tibidabo funicular station and take the funicular railroad to the top)

### SAVVY **TRAVELER**

Tibidabo's amusement park opens daily in July and August, but at other times check the website. When the park is open, bus T2A runs from Plaça de Catalunya to Tibidabo. Don't forget a picnic, as you can take food and drink inside.

The views from Tibidabo, the city's highest hill, add to the attractions of the amusement park.

**CAMP NOU TO TIBIDABO**

# Monestir de Pedralbes

*Be entranced by this medieval monastery turned museum tucked away at the end of a cobblestone lane in upscale Pedralbes.*

**Slender Catalan Gothic columns support the cloisters around the verdant garden.**

Climb the hill through the Pedralbes neighborhood, past smart apartment buildings, and turn into a small lane to discover another era at the Monestir de Pedralbes. Founded in 1326 by Queen Elisenda, the fourth wife of Jaume II, the church and monastery were built in Catalan Gothic style (see pp. 56–57). The three-tiered cloisters surround a garden overflowing with herbs, flowers, and cypress and palm trees. This peaceful place evokes the contemplative lives of the nuns of the Order of Saint Clare who have lived here over the centuries.

## ■ Església de Pedralbes

Begin your visit in the church adjacent to the monastery. Inside, wide arches and numerous columns engraved with the heralds of the kings of Aragon support a single nave. Be sure to see Queen Elisenda de Montcada's carved marble tomb and the altarpiece by the great Catalan Gothic painter Jaume Huguet (1412–1492). Walk a few steps from the church to the cloister, then follow the signposted route.

## ■ Art & Solitude

One of the first rooms you see, the **Capella de Sant Miquel,** was also the abbess's day cell. The walls of the chapel are decorated with two frescoes by the revered Catalan painter Jaume Ferrer Bassa (1285–1348). Continue around the cloister to see the tiny cells used by nuns for daily prayer. They offer a glimpse of the solitude and hardship, as well as the spirituality, of traditional monastic life. Muse for a moment on this pattern of life, still led by the nuns now living in a nearby house. Then walk up the stairs to the next floor.

## ■ Museum & Everyday Life

The former dormitory, now a light-filled museum, displays many religious artifacts, paintings, and furniture the nuns collected. View more cells used for prayer or as bedrooms, before returing to the ground floor and visiting the dining room and kitchen. Here, the long tables and large stone sinks recall the nuns' communal life.

## ■ Gardens

Do not miss the chance to sit for a few minutes in the tranquil garden. Visit in the middle of the day, when large palm trees provide welcome shade from the heat of the city.

Baixada del Monestir, 9 • www.museuhistoria.bcn.es • 932 563 434 • €€ • Closed Mon., Jan. 1, May 1, June 24, Dec. 25 • FGC: Reina Elisenda

CAMP NOU TO TIBIDABO

# Soccer

Visitors to Barcelona cannot help noticing that the city is soccer crazy. Pictures of soccer players decorate shop windows; soccer shirts hang from washing lines; kids kick balls around the backstreets. But Futbol Club Barcelona, the city's world-famous soccer club, has an importance that extends far beyond sports, serving as a cherished symbol of Catalan identity and a focus for political loyalties. As the club's slogan claims, it is truly: "More than a club."

**CAMP NOU TO TIBIDABO**

Fans of Futbol Club Barcelona (above), wearing face paint in Barça's colors, celebrate as their club wins the Spanish League in 2011. Holding aloft the prize cup, the team enjoy their victory (right).

## Heritage & Identity

To understand the special status of FC Barcelona in Catalonia you need to plunge back in history. In the period of the Franco dictatorship, from 1939 to 1975, Catalans often expressed their identity by supporting their local soccer club—FC Barcelona. At a time when Franco banned the Catalan flag and language, the Barcelona stadium became the only place where Catalan could be spoken openly. Matches against Real Madrid, the team favored by the Franco regime, took on a significance they have never lost. To this day, Catalan separatists celebrate a victory over Real as if it were a successful rebellion against Spain's central government.

## The People's Club

An unusual ownership structure cements the bond between the club and the city. About 170,000 members have money invested in the club and elect its president. Most members are local soccer fans, although not all—Pope John Paul II was a famous honorary member. Unlike most professional soccer clubs, Barcelona had no commercial sponsorship until recently. Mounting debts forced this policy to be abandoned in 2011. It remains one of the richest sports clubs in the world, valued at more than $1 billion and attracting on average almost 80,000 paying customers for its home matches.

## Loyal Fans

Catalans do not have a monopoly on supporting Barcelona—people from across Spain make up a large part of its fan base, and it has 1,300 fan clubs worldwide. The popularity of the club has brought it widespread fame and great wealth. But the people of Barcelona know their team will always be more than just another rich, successful soccer club. FC Barcelona belongs to the city and to them.

# City Views

Of all the stunning views of the Mediterranean, those from the city's highest point are arguably the best. Tibidabo forms one of these high points, but this vertiginous hill cannot compete with the other high spot, a modern communications tower. Enjoy city views from castles and cable cars to parks and luxury bars.

### ■ MIRADOR DE LA TORRE DE COLLSEROLA

The reward for a long trip up Tibidabo to the Torre de Collserola includes sweeping views from city to sea, plus great modern engineering. This svelte 945-foot-high (288 m) communications tower designed by British architect Sir Norman Foster debuted for the 1992 Summer Olympics. Do not miss the tenth-floor observation deck (*mirador*).

Vallvidrera al Tibidabo • www.torredecollserola .com • 934 069 354 • Opening times, which are the same as for Tibidabo, vary; check at www .tibidabo • Av. Tibidabo (then Tramvia Blau or 196 bus to Tibidabo funicular station and take the funicular railroad to the top)

### ■ TEMPLE EXPIATORI DEL SAGRAT COR

Near Tibidabo's amusement park (see p. 151), this church dominates the mountain with a statue of Christ at the top. Built by Enric Sagnier in a mixture of styles, the church has two elevators to the roof. From there, climb the stairs up to the statue for top-of-the-world views.

Tibidabo • FGC: Av. Tibidabo (then Tramvia Blau or 196 bus to Tibidabo funicular station and take the funicular railroad to the top)

### ■ ECLIPSE BAR

Go to the waterfront and soak up the jet set ambiance of this club on the 26th floor of the W hotel (see p. 125). The minimalist décor complements floor to ceiling windows framing sea vistas.

Plaça de la Rosa dels Vents, 1 • www.w -barcelona.es • 932 952 800 • Metro: Barceloneta

### ■ MIRADOR DE COLOM

For views over the waterfront and the bustling old city, ride the elevator in this iconic landmark (see p. 83) to a *mirador*.

Plaça Portal de la Pau • www.barcelonaturisme .com • 932 853 832 • € • Closed Jan. 1, Dec. 25 • Metro: Drassanes

**The view from Tibidabo's illuminated fairground makes it a perfect destination on a clear night.**

### ■ TRANSBORDADOR AERI

Near the waterfront, hop on a cable car (see p. 84) from Sant Sebastià beach or the World Trade Center, or ride from Montjuïc, and enjoy bird's-eye views over Barcelona. Visitors have enjoyed these short jaunts for more than 80 years.

Moll de Barcelona • www.telefericodebarcelona .com • 934 414 820 • €€ • Closed Dec. 25 • Metro: Barceloneta or Drassanes

### ■ PARK GÜELL

Gaudí's magical park (see pp. 131–133) overlooks the city from the Gràcia district in northern Barcelona. Enjoy cityscape views from the famous serpentine bench on the upper level, then follow the paths to the top of the hill for even grander views.

Olot, 5 • Metro: Lesseps; Bus: 24,31, 32

### ■ CASTELL DE MONTJUÏC

On the peak of Montjuïc perches this 17th-century fortress (see p. 167). Vistas stretch over the sea: To the left, ferries and fishing boats sail to the Balearic Islands; to the right, Zona Franca houses the cruise ship terminal and commercial port.

Ctra. de Montjuïc, 66 • www.bcn.cat • 932 564 445 • Metro: Espanya or Paral·lel and funicular

# Montjuïc

Climb this uneven hill rising above the port to the south of the city and discover cultural centers and sports arenas set between landscaped paths. Montjuïc has been used for ceremonies and recreation for centuries; the earliest Iberian communities settled on the hill and the Romans performed rituals on the site. More recently, Montjuïc hosted the 1929 International Exhibition and the 1992 Summer Olympics. These events left a legacy of sports venues and art installations that have been developed over the years. The Olympic stadium holds major competitions and concerts, while cultural centers include the world-class Joan Miró Foundation and the CaixaForum contemporary exhibition space. Gardens bloom across the hillside, making Montjuïc a vast green space for exercise and leisure, with views in every direction. At the foot of the northern side, you can explore Poble Sec, a popular neighborhood with a lively nightlife and many choices for tapas or dining.

◗ **Built in 1929, Poble Espanyol displays a range of architecture from across Spain, like this Mudéjar-style tower from Utebo in Zaragoza.**

# Montjuïc

*A hillside walk takes in Olympic sports, elegant art, and beautiful gardens, with panoramic views of the city and sea.*

**3 Pavelló Mies van der Rohe** (see p. 163) Designed in 1929, this minimalist building still looks modern today. Walk up Av. Ferrer i Guàrdia to Poble Espanyol.

**2 CaixaFòrum** (see pp. 162–163) Make your way to this cultural center to see a range of exhibitions and events. Then cross the road to the Mies van der Rohe Pavilion.

**1 Plaça d' Espanya** (see p. 162) Cross this square to the Venetian Towers, the entrance to the 1929 International Exhibition. At the end of Av. Reina Maria Cristina, turn right onto Av. Ferrer i Guàrdia.

**4 Poble Espanyol** (see p. 164) This visitor attraction, built as a Spanish village, offers entertainment and cafés. Make your way back past Pavelló Mies van der Rohe and ride the escalators up to the Museu Nacional.

**5 Museu Nacional** (see pp. 168–169) The monumental Palau Nacional houses the National Museum, covering 1,000 years of art. The terrace café has one of the best views of the city. Walk around the building for escalators up to Av. de l'Estadi.

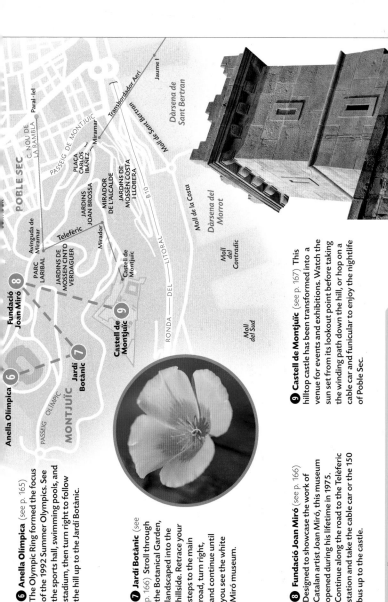

**6 Anella Olímpica** (see p. 165)
The Olympic Ring formed the focus of the 1992 Summer Olympics. See the sports hall, swimming pools, and stadium, then turn right to follow the hill up to the Jardí Botànic.

**7 Jardí Botànic** (see p. 166) Stroll through the Botanical Garden, landscaped into the hillside. Retrace your steps to the main road, turn right, and continue until you see the white Miró museum.

**8 Fundació Joan Miró** (see p. 166)
Designed to showcase the work of Catalan artist Joan Miró, this museum opened during his lifetime in 1975. Continue along the road to the Teleféric station and take the cable car or the 150 bus up to the castle.

**9 Castell de Montjuïc** (see p. 167) This hilltop castle has been transformed into a venue for events and exhibitions. Watch the sun set from its lookout point before taking the winding path down the hill, or hop on a cable car and funicular to enjoy the nightlife of Poble Sec.

**MONTJUÏC DISTANCE: 3.7 MILES (6 KM)**
**TIME: APPROX. 9 HOURS METRO START: ESPANYA**

**MONTJUÏC**

Map labels: POBLE SEC, Paral·lel, C. NOU DE LA RAMBLA, PASSEIG DE MONTJUÏC, Avinguda de Miramar, Teleféric, PARC LARIBAL, Anella Olímpica 6, Fundació Joan Miró 8, Jardí Botànic 7, MONTJUÏC, PASSEIG OLÍMPIC, JARDINS DE MOSSÈN CINTO VERDAGUER, Mirador, JARDINS JOAN BROSSA, MIRADOR DE L'ALCALDE, JARDINS DE MOSSÈN COSTA I LLOBERA, PLAÇA CARLOS IBÁÑEZ, Miramar, Transbordador Aeri, Castell de Montjuïc 9, Castell de Montjuïc, RONDA — DEL — LITORAL, B10, Moll de la Costa, Moll de Sant Bertran, Dàrsena de Sant Bertran, Dàrsena del Morrot, Moll del Contradic, Moll del Sud, Jaume I

## Plaça d'Espanya

**1** Traffic converges at this busy junction, and crowds stream across the area to take an escalator or climb the steps up Montjuïc. Locals heading for art exhibitions mingle with business people going to trade fairs held along Avinguda Reina Maria Cristina. Pause to appreciate the square's elaborate central fountain, sculpted by Josep Maria Jujol, one of Gaudí's close collaborators, as an homage to Spain for the 1929 International Exhibition.

Intersection of Carrer de Sants, Gran Via de les Corts Catalanes, and Av. del Parral · lel • Metro: Espanya

## CaixaForum

**2** Puig i Cadafalch, a key *modernista* architect, designed the prize-winning textile factory, Casa Ramona, in 1911. In its new life as a cultural center, CaixaForum has become a prized addition to

The colorful "Splat" in the entrance to CaixaForum sets the scene for the art you will see there.

Barcelona's art scene. A high-quality program of temporary exhibitions usually includes one area with pieces from "la Caixa" Foundation's huge contemporary art collection, the largest in Spain. As you arrive at the new, sculpted metal and glass entrance designed by Japanese architect Arata Isozaki, an escalator sweeps you down past dazzling white marble walls to a hall presided over by Sol LeWitt's specially commissioned mural **"Splat."** Visit a selection of the exhibitions or shop in the bookstore. Be sure to explore the exterior walkways upstairs, running past the original redbrick towers with their bright blue ceramic and glass details. They are virtually unchanged since the building was used as a textile factory. This interesting building also provides a perfect venue for a varied program of concerts from classical to world music, or late-night summer sessions.

Av. Francesc Ferrer i Guàrdia, 6–8 • www.obrasocial .lacaixa.es • 934 768 600 • € • Closed Jan. 1 and 6, Dec. 25 • Metro: Espanya

## Pavelló Mies van der Rohe

**3** The Mies van der Rohe Pavilion encapsulates the "less is more" maxim attributed to him and has become an iconic example of his work. The original building was designed in 1929 as Germany's pavilion for the International Exhibition held in Barcelona. Considered the father of modern architecture, Mies van der Rohe saw the pavilion as an opportunity to express the ideas of simple lines, uncluttered space, and the merging of interior and exterior. Although the original temporary building was demolished in 1930, Barcelona architects faithfully recreated the pavilion in 1986, using the same construction materials, such as red onyx, green marble, and steel. Visit the house to see Van der Rohe's white leather **"Barcelona Chair,"** now a modern design icon.

**The minimalist lines of the Mies van der Rohe Pavilion show off the polished stone.**

Av. Francesc Ferrer i Guàrdia, 7 • www.miesbcn.com • 934 234 016 • €€ • Metro: Espanya

**MONTJUÏC**

**Some of the 117 full-scale buildings that have been re-created at Poble Espanyol**

## Poble Espanyol

④ As large as many villages in Spain, with life-size buildings representing the country's regional architectural styles, the Spanish Village has been a popular attraction since it opened in the 1929 International Exhibition. Whitewashed houses from Andalucía jostle against noble family houses from Castilla, a Romanesque-style church from Catalunya, and a Plaza Mayor, the main square of any village. Artists work in the buildings, so you can watch glass blowers, weavers, and ceramicists, then buy their crafts. The village also displays the Fran Daurel art collection, which includes work by prominent Spaniards from Picasso to contemporary artists. The sculpture garden, with 27 works, makes a pleasant walk. At night the village comes alive with restaurants, bars, and a flamenco show; a younger set head for the discos—one in the open air.

Av. de Francesc Ferrer i Guàrdia, 13 • www.poble-espanyol.com • 935 086 324 • €€€
• Metro: Espanya

## Museu Nacional

**5** See pp. 168–169.

Palau Nacional, Parc de Montjuïc • www.mnac.cat • 936 220 376 • €€€
• Closed Mon. (except public holidays), Jan. 1, May 1, Dec. 25 • Metro: Espanya

## Anella Olímpica

**6** The 1992 Summer Olympics became a turning point in Barcelona's recent history when new infrastructure and dazzling architecture impressed audiences around the globe and brought the city to the world's attention. In the complex of buildings, known as the Olympic Ring, the **Palau Sant Jordi** *(Passeig Olímpic, 5–7)* designed by Arata Isozaki takes center stage. It remains in use for indoor sports events, but it also holds up to 24,000 people for mega rock concerts. The venue's vast ceramic-tiled roof, larger than a soccer field, had to be built on the ground, then hauled into place. Spanish architect Santiago Calatrava's communications tower dramatically points 616 feet (188 m) into the sky next to the **Picornell swimming pools** (see p. 172), where you can have an Olympic dip. A landscaped esplanade and gardens connect the venues and offer views of the city and sea. The main stadium, **Estadi Olímpic Lluís Companys** *(Passeig Olímpic, 17–19)*, built for the 1936 games that were due to be held in Spain but were moved to Germany with the outbreak of civil war, was overhauled for 1992. The venue held 65,000 people for track events as well as the opening and closing ceremonies. Today, the stadium is open to the public and hosts soccer, track-and-field meetings, rugby, and rock concerts.

Parc de Montjuïc, Av. de l'Estadi, between INEFC (Sports University) and Estadi Olímpic • www.barcelonaturisme.com • Metro: Espanya or Paral·lel and funicular

### GOOD **EATS**

■ **ELCHE**
The Valencian owners of this traditional restaurant prepare authentic rice dishes like *paella,* which originated in Valencia, and *arròs negre d'elx amb calamarsets i carxofes* (black rice with baby squid and artichokes). **Vila i Vilà, 71, 934 413 089, €€€**

■ **FUNDACIÓ JOAN MIRÓ**
Lunch on light Mediterranean dishes in a restaurant with garden views. Or admire Miró sculptures over a snack in the peaceful courtyard. **Avinguda de Miramar, 1, 933 290 768, €€**

■ **QUIMET & QUIMET**
Stop for classic tapas at this bar run by the fourth generation of one family. Push through the crush to order *montaditos,* bread piled with seasonal morsels, or a *combinado,* small dishes with a tasty selection of food. **Poeta Cabanyes, 25, 934 423 142, €€**

## Jardí Botànic

**7** Small but beautiful, the Botanical Garden opened in 1999 on a previously unkempt part of the hill, once full of shanty houses. Away from the city bustle, a well laid-out and signposted path offers spectacular views over the Olympic complex to the **Garraf hills.** The walk takes you past the indigenous flora of the world's regions with a Mediterranean climate—parts of Australia, Chile, California, and South Africa, as well as the Mediterranean basin. Imagine you have traveled far afield by visiting the abundant laurel forest of the Canaries with curious species like St. John's Bread and Climbing Butcher's Broom.

Dr. Font i Quer, 2 • www.jardibotanic.bcn.cat • 932 564 160 • € • Closed Jan. 1, May 1, June 24, Dec. 25 • Metro: Espanya or Paral·lel and funicular

## Fundació Joan Miró

**8** Born in the middle of the old town in Barcelona, Joan Miró became a leading light in the surrealist movement. His Catalan friend, the rationalist architect Josep Lluís Sert, designed this bright white building with exceptionally luminous interior spaces. Skylights and a central patio flood light over Miró's work, including 200 paintings, 180 sculptures, and thousands of drawings, as well as ceramic and textile work, such as the colorful wall-hanging **"Tapís,"** designed especially for the building. Works by Miró's contemporaries, including Marcel Duchamp, Max Ernst, and Juli González, also feature in the collection. Alexander Calder donated his mobile sculpture, **"Mercury Fountain,"** to the foundation in tribute to his friendship with Miró. The foundation also has a good reputation for holding incisive temporary exhibitions of contemporary art.

Parc de Montjuïc • www.fundaciomiro-bcn.org • 934 439 470 • €€€ • Closed Mon., Jan. 1, Dec. 25–26 • Metro: Espanya or Paral·lel and funicular

## Castell de Montjuïc

**9**   The castle tops the summit of the 600-foot–high (183 m) Montjuïc hill. Once a symbol of Madrid's oppression for many Catalans, it was built during the 17th-century war waged between Catalonia and Felipe IV of Spain. The castle was later attacked by Bourbon troops and rebuilt in the late 18th century with its current layout, deep moat, and sturdy buttresses. The castle witnessed many imprisonments and executions, particularly during the Civil War: Lluís Companys, President of the Generalitat, was shot here in 1940. In 2007, the castle was ceremoniously returned to Catalonia, and now the red and yellow Catalan flag flies over the handsome building. Inside, an exhibition explains the history of the castle and hill. During the summer open-air cinema season, you can picnic under the stars. Return via cable car and funicular or enjoy a walk down through a series of well-designed gardens.

Ctra. de Montjuïc, 66 • www.bcn.cat • 932 564 445
• Metro: Espanya or Paral·lel and funicular

MONTJUÏC

A relic of its military past, this gun occupies a prime position at Montjuïc Castle.

# Museu Nacional

*The imposing National Museum displays the world's most important collection of Catalan art from the medieval period to the 20th century.*

**The museum's terrace overlooks the city and the Quatre Barres symbol of Catalan nationalism.**

The National Museum exhibits the treasures of Catalan art in the main building of the 1929 World Exhibition, the Palau Nacional. Designed to impress, the building stands imperiously at the top of the wide stairway of Avinguda de la Reina Maria Cristina, with views across the city. The museum's collection spans over a thousand years, from medieval to modern, and includes frescoes and furniture, as well as paintings. Each time period is clearly separated, so choose the section that interests you most to explore first.

■ Romanesque

The Romanesque galleries contain some of the best works in Europe, notably well-preserved frescoes rescued from decaying churches in the Pyrenees. Paintings from the 11th–13th centuries that once covered whole walls, such as **"Christ in Majesty"** from a church in Taüll, were removed to be preserved and displayed here. Painted wood sculptures also feature in the collection including **"Descent from the Cross,"** also from Taüll.

■ Gothic

The riches that poured into Barcelona during the Gothic era were spent on adorning churches with works of art. The museum now houses many of these works, including masterpeices such as the **"Nativity"** by Lluís Borrassà from Santes Creus monastery. As the Gothic movement spread from France and Italy, it influenced the work of Catalan masters such as Jaume Huguet and Bernat Martorell. Their work hangs alongside Italian paintings, including Fra Angelico's **"Madonna of Humility,"** from the Thyssen-Bornemisza collection.

IN **THE KNOW**

**The Òleum museum restaurant, situated in the room where King Alfonso XIII inaugurated the 1929 World Exhibiton, serves good Mediterranean dishes. Make an evening reservation *(932 890 679, Tues.–Sat.)* to watch the city light up as you dine. A new roof terrace café gives even loftier panoramic views.**

■ Renaissance & Baroque

These galleries showcase international artists, such as Rubens and Titian, as well as works by Spanish artists El Greco, Velázquez, and Zurbarán. Do not miss Zurbarán's powerful **"St. Francis of Assisi According to Pope Nicholas V's Vision."**

■ The Modern Collection

Catalan artists of the 19th and 20th centuries are not well known outside Spain, but paintings by Marià Fortuny, Nonell, and Rusiñol are worth viewing. Visit the ***Modernista*** section to see interior decoration and furniture by Gaudí, and sculptures such as Josep Llimona's **"Desolation."** The museum also has collections of photographs, prints, drawings, and stamps.

Palau Nacional, Parc de Montjuïc • www.mnac.cat • 936 220 376 • €€€ • Closed Mon. (except public holidays), Jan. 1, May 1, Dec. 25 • Metro: Espanya

# Artists in the City

Home to avant-garde and surrealist writers and artists, Barcelona has a reputation for creativity that dates from the 19th century and continues to thrive in the streets and galleries today. The sleazy lanes of the old town and clear light of the countryside and sea inspired some of the most imaginative modern artists—Picasso, Miró, and Tàpies—all of whom have museums dedicated to their work.

MONTJUÏC

The unmistakable colors of Joan Miró in one of his last pieces, the 70-foot-high (21 m) "Dona i Ocell" ("Woman and Bird"; above). It stands in Parc de Joan Miró (see p. 59). The trio of artists—Miró, Picasso, and Dalí (right)—all had strong links with Barcelona and Catalonia.

## Patronage & Wealth

The industrial hothouse of mid-19th-century Barcelona created wealthy patrons for art, as well as a generation of young men with a family income that allowed them to paint. These artists worked in Barcelona at around the same time as the Postimpressionists in Paris, and the link between the two cities has always been strong. Ramon Casas, whose father had grown rich in Cuba, was the leading *modernista* artist and made his home in the city. He funded the **Els Quatre Gats bar** (see p. 104) where artists met, married a flower girl from La Rambla, and lived in **Casa Casas** (now the designer store, Vinçon; see pp. 31, 109).

His great friend, Santiago Rusiñol, the son of a wealthy textile manufacturer, was drawn to the nearby fishing village of Sitges. There, Rusiñol invited artists to his studio, now the **Museu Cau Ferrat** (*Sitges, 938 940 364*). Rusiñol in turn influenced Pablo Picasso, who arrived in Barcelona as a teenager when his father was appointed to teach at the art school in the Barri Gòtic. There, his family became friends with Joan Miró's family.

## Catalan Influence

Although now known for its modern artists, Barcelona did not always appreciate avant-garde art. At Miró's first solo exhibition, in the Dalmau Gallery, his colorful compositions were vilified. Although Picasso left for Paris, Barcelona's influence lingered in his work. His cubist "Les Demoiselles d'Avignon" (1907), depicting prostitutes in the Barri Gòtic's Carrer Avinyó, marks a pivotal point in the development of modern art.

Catalan artists broke new ground, while always acknowledging a debt to their heritage. Picasso and Dalí admired Velázquez, while Antoni Tàpies, Barcelona's best known late 20th-century painter, claimed inspiration from Catalan Romanesque paintings, though his work is entirely abstract.

## SALVADOR **DALÍ**

Three Dalí museums in northern Catalonia can be visited in a day:

**Casa-Museu,** Port-Lligat, near Cadaqués. Created from two fishermen's cottages it became Dalí's home for more than 50 years. **www .salvador-dali.org**

**Gala Dalí Castle,** Púbol. Bought by Dalí for his wife, Gala. This medieval castle gives an insight into their final years together. **www .salvador-dali.org**

**Theatre-Museum,** Figueres. A surrealist work of art where Dalí is buried. **www.salvador-dali.org**

# Sporty Barcelona

Barcelona has been a sports center for many years, with the oldest tennis club in Spain, a world-class classic yacht race, and a Grand Prix circuit, in addition to the Olympic legacy. For many visitors, sporting Barcelona now means more than just watching a Barça soccer match; it means participating, too.

■ On the Road

Long-distance street cycling is popular in Spain, and the **Alto de Montjuïc,** a 1.2-mile-high (1.9 km) route with an average gradient of 4:8, challenges the most experienced cyclists.

Formula One Grand Prix cars and motorcycles raced on the Montjuïc circuit until the1970s, and classic bike and car rallies are still held here. The modern Grand Prix circuit, the **Circuit de Catalunya** (*Mas "La Moreneta" PD, 27, Montmeló, 935 719 700*), located to the north of the city, offers tours throughout the year.

■ In & On the Water

Montjuïc's Olympic pools at **Piscines Picornell** (*Av. de l'Estadi, 30, 934 234 041*) host championship events and are open to the public for swimming. High divers will head to the **Piscina Municipal de Montjuïc** (*Avinguda de Miramar, 31, 934 430 046*), open only

in August, where you may dive and swim in the pools while enjoying the dramatic views over Barcelona.

Learn how to sail at the **Olympic Port:** The Centre Municipal de Vela has details (*Moll de Gregal, s/n, Port Olímpic, 932 257 940*). The **Royal Barcelona Yacht Club** in Port Vell (*Moll d'Espanya, s/n, 932 216 521*), with 200 berths, also has a sailing school. The club organizes 12 regattas each year, including one for international classic boats in July and a round-the-world race.

■ Tennis

On Montjuïc, rent a tennis court for a game at **Pompeia Club Tennis** (*Carrer de la Fuxarda, 2–16, 933 251 348*) or **Club Natació** (*Segura, s/n, 933 318 288*). Local hero Catalan Rafael Nadal, born in Mallorca, has won the ATP Barcelona Open many times. The championship is played near the Tibidabo area on the clay courts of the

Races on the Grand Prix circuit draw crowds to the Circuit de Catalunya just outside the city.

**Real Club de Tenis Barcelona** (*Bosch i Gimpera, 5–13, 932 037 852*), a private club founded in 1899. Tennis is also played at the **Real Club de Polo de Barcelona** (*Av. del Dr. Marañón, 19–31, 934 480 400*), the city's polo club.

### ■ FC BARCELONA

Camp Nou is home to FC Barcelona (see pp. 154–155), and the fans' song "El Cant de Barça" fills the streets of the city during any important match, notably with their archrival Real Madrid. But the venue hosts other activities and teams as well. Barcelona's women's soccer team was national champion in 2012, and its rugby teams were founded in 1924, four years before the football club.

## BULLFIGHTING

Barcelona's Monumental bullring, a beautiful, tile-and-brick Mudéjar building, held the last bullfight in Catalonia in September 2011, when the province became the first in Spain to ban the spectacle. The future of the venue is uncertain. Barcelona's other bullring, Las Arenas, has been converted into a shopping mall (see p. 162).

### ■ ICE-SKATING

Visit FC Barcelona's sports hall, the Palau Blaugrana, to try ice-skating on the public **rink** (*Av. Joan XXIII, s/n, 934 963 631*). Barcelona's ice hockey, roller hockey, handball, and basketball teams also train at the sports hall.

**PART 3**

# Travel Essentials

# TRAVEL **ESSENTIALS**

## PLANNING YOUR TRIP

### When To Go
The city is popular year-round, although some times are busier than others. Peak periods include Easter week, Christmas to New Year, and the summer.

The quietest period is from **December to late February** (except for Christmas and New Year). **February's Carnival** (at its most raucous in Sitges—see p. 91) marks the end of winter for many.

If you want to avoid the strangulating heat of the summer months, the best time to visit is **late April through June.** Most locals take their vacations in **August,** and the city takes on a strangely empty air as many shops, restaurants, and bars shut down. Banks and public offices work on reduced morning-only timetables. The vacuum is filled by those Barcelonians who choose to stay behind to enjoy the summer theater season or local street festivals, and by foreign visitors to the city.

### Climate
Extremes of summer heat and humidity aside, Barcelona basks in a moderate Mediterranean climate. Spring tends to be unstable, and you never know if the weather is going to be cold, wet, or hot. As early summer approaches—from late April through June—the days become brighter and are sometimes hot. July and August are the hottest months.

Traditionally Barcelona gets a soaking from late September to October, while November, although cool, is often dry and sunny. Winters are chilly but not excessively cold.

### Insurance
Take out enough travel insurance to cover emergency medical treatment, loss or theft, and repatriation.

### Passports
U.S. and Canadian citizens can stay in Spain for up to three months with just a valid passport. No visa is required.

## HOW TO GET TO BARCELONA

### Airport
Barcelona has one airport: **El Prat** (902 404 704), 7.5 miles (12 km) southwest of Barcelona.

Getting into town is easy. The **Rodalies** (Cercanías, in Spanish) local train service runs from a station about a five-minute walk along an overpass between terminals A and B. Main stops include Estació Sants and Passeig de Gràcia. Trains run every half hour from 6 a.m.–10:29 p.m. (19 minutes to Sants; 24 minutes to Passeig de Gràcia). Departures from Sants to the airport are from 5:33 a.m.–10:55 p.m.; from Passeig de Gràcia they're five minutes earlier. Tickets cost €3.80 (for a single ride) and are available from the ticket office or a machine at the station.

The **A1 Aerobús** service runs to Plaça de Catalunya via Plaça d'Espanya every 8–15 minutes from 6 a.m. to 1 a.m. Departures from Plaça de Catalunya are 5:30 a.m.–12:15 a.m. The trip takes about 40 minutes. A taxi to central Barcelona should cost around €22–€25.

### Train or Bus
The main train station for national and international routes is Estació Sants, on Plaça dels Països Catalans. For information, contact the Spanish railway **Renfe** (www.renfe.es, 902 240 202). Most national bus services arrive and depart from Estació del Nord (Carrer d'Alí Bei, 80, 902 303 222). Many international services depart from Estació d'Autobusos de Sants, alongside the Estació Sants train station.

## GETTING AROUND

### Public Transportation
Barcelona's buses, metro, and suburban trains are integrated in a single-ticket system under the **Autoritat del Transport Metropolità (ATM).** The network extends well beyond the city into six zones, but most sights are within zone 1. A single ride costs €2.00. Targetes are multiple-trip transport tickets sold at most city-center metro stations and some newspaper stands. Targeta T-10 (€9.80) gives you ten rides. You can catch a combination of metro, bus, and train within

1 hour and 15 minutes from the time you validate each ride on boarding. Targeta T-DIA (€7.25) gives unlimited travel for a day. The Targeta T-50/30 is for 50 trips within 30 days (€32.20). The T-Mes is a monthly pass for unlimited journeys (€52.75).

For public transportation information, you can call 010 or 932 051 515 (for FGC trains only). **TMB,** the public transit authority, runs four customer service centers: in Estació Sants (the mainline Renfe station) and at the metro stops of Universitat, Diagonal, and Sagrada Família.

### Metro
The metro has six lines, numbered and color-coded, and provides the simplest way of getting around town. Take care of your pockets on the metro, as pickpockets operate there, especially in the rush-hour crush. Operating hours are: 5 a.m.– midnight, Sun. through Thurs.; 5 a.m.–2 a.m. Fri.; 5 a.m.–5 a.m. Sat. and public holidays.

### FGC (Ferrocarrils de la Generalitat de Catalunya)
This is a supplementary suburban train system with a couple of lines that run through central Barcelona. Operating hours are: 5 a.m.– 11 p.m. Sun. through Thurs., and 5 a.m.–2 a.m. Fri. and Sat.

### Rodalies/Cercanías
Run by Renfe, these trains fan out from the city to nearby towns, such as Sitges and Vilafranca del Penedès. Operating hours are: 5 a.m.– 11:30 p.m. (some lines close earlier), stopping at Sants, Plaça de Catalunya, Passeig de Gràcia, and some other stations.

### Bus
The city has an extensive bus network, although the metro is faster and more convenient. Night buses are an exception, but they operate on limited routes, starting or passing through Plaça de Catalunya. **TMB** (daytime service) Operating hours are: 5 a.m.–11 p.m. (times vary, so be sure to check).
**TMB Nitbus** (night service) Operating hours are: 11 p.m.– 5 a.m. (some services end earlier).

### Taxi
Barcelona's black-and-yellow cabs are reasonably abundant and, by European standards, good value. Generally, taxi drivers follow the rules and turn on the meter. Note that the final fare may have extras thrown in (for instance, for large items of luggage and for driving to the airport). Fares go up marginally between 9 p.m. and 7 a.m. on weekends and on holidays. You can hail a cab on the street or pick one up at a cab rank. Look for a green light on the roof, which means the cab is free. Sometimes you'll also see a *lliure* or *libre* sign in the windshield (Catalan and Spanish for "unoccupied"). You can call a taxi (932 250 000, 933 300 300, 933 001 100, or 933 222 222). General information is available by calling 010.

### Tours & Sightseeing
#### Bicycle Tours
Several organizations offer these tours, including: **Bike Tours Barcelona** (Carrer de l'Esparteria, 3, www.biketoursbarcelona.com, 932 682 105) and **Fat Tire Bike Tours** (Carrer dels Escudellers, 48, www .fattirebiketoursbarcelona.com, 933 013 612).

#### Boat Tours
Half-hour boat trips with the **Golondrinas** service (see p. 82; 934 423 106) chug around the harbor from Moll de les Drassanes near the Monument a Colom (€5). The same people run a 90-minute trip to Port Olímpic (€10.50) on a glass-bottom catamaran.

#### Bus Tours
The **Bus Turístic** service links tourist sights on two circuits (37 stops). It is a hop-on, hop-off service, and tickets, available on the bus, are €19 for one day's unlimited rides or €23 for two consecutive days. For city tours contact **Julià Tours** (Ronda de la Universitat, 5, 933 176 454) or **Pullmantur** (Gran Via de les Corts Catalanes, 645, 933 180 241).

#### Walking Tours
A walking tour of the Barri Gòtic (€11) starts at 10 a.m. on Saturday and Sunday mornings at the main tourist office on Plaça de Catalunya. The tourist office also has similar tours covering some *modernista* sights, walking in Picasso's footsteps, and a gourmet tour.

**TRAVEL ESSENTIALS**

## PRACTICAL ADVICE

### Electricity
Spanish circuits (mostly) use 220 volts. American appliances need adaptor plugs, and those that operate on 110 volts will also need a transformer.

### Money Matters
**Interchange** foreign exchange service *(La Rambla, 74, 933 427 311)*. Metro: Liceu. American Express clients only.

Barcelona is full of banks, and most change foreign currency (look for signs saying *canvi* or *cambio*, or displays with the day's exchange rates). You are better off changing money in a bank, but if you need to change money outside of banking hours, currency exchanges abound in the center. Check the commission and the day's exchange rate.

The currency of Spain is the euro (€); one euro equals 100 cents. Coins are of 1, 2, 5, 10, 20, and 50 cents and 1 and 2 euros. Bills are 5, 10, 20, 50, 100, 200, and 500 euros.

The best sources of currency with a credit/debit card are the ATMs *(caixer automàtic/ cajero automático)*, outside many banks. Most major cards will work, but you should check with your bank or credit card supplier that your PIN is valid overseas. Cash advances will incur a transaction charge.

### Opening Times
Bank opening times tend to vary considerably, but as a rule you should try to do your banking between 8 a.m. and 2 p.m. Mon.–Fri. Some banks stay open until 4 p.m. (or occasionally later). Virtually all close by 2 p.m. in the hot summer months.

Bar hours are much more flexible, and the distinction between where you have a cup of coffee or settle for a night's drinking is vague. Many bars aimed at daytime and after-work customers will be closed by 10 p.m. Quite a few in the center stay open later, and in many more alcohol-orientated bars it is quite possible to get a coffee too. Restaurants are generally open for lunch 1 p.m.–4 p.m. and for dinner 9 p.m.–midnight.

Store hours vary, but many open Mon.–Fri. about 10 a.m. –8 p.m., often closing around 2–4 p.m. for lunch. Many open on Saturdays, too, but sometimes only until 2 p.m.

Churches and public offices often close at lunchtime.

### Post Offices
The main post office branch *(Plaça d'Antoni López, 08002, 902 197 197)* is open Mon.– Sat. 8:30 a.m.–10 p.m., Sun. noon–10 p.m. Local branches are open Mon.–Fri. 8:30 a.m.– 2 p.m. A handful open Mon.– Fri. 8:30 a.m.–8:30 p.m., Sat. 9:30 a.m.–1 p.m.

Known in Catalan as **Correus** (Correos in Spanish), the Spanish postal service has branches across the city, although few in central Barcelona. For ordinary mail, you can also purchase stamps from *estancos* (tobacconists). Look for the yellow-on-maroon *tabacos* signs. Mail forwarded to you at the central post office should be addressed to you at *Lista de Correos, 08080 Barcelona.* Take your passport along as ID to pick up any mail.

Yellow *bústies/buzones* (mailboxes) are located at post offices and across town. Addresses in Barcelona can be quite complex, reflecting the location of apartments in various parts of any given building. "C/ Carme 14, 3°D Int." probably looks utterly indecipherable. It means 14 Carme Street, 3rd floor, right hand *(dreta/derecha)*, interior (where there are several sets of floors, some might be well inside, off the street, and look onto an internal courtyard).

### Telephones
All Spanish phone numbers have nine digits. The first two or three digits (93 in the case of Barcelona) indicate the province but must always be dialed, even if you are calling from next door. Numbers beginning with 6 are cell-phone numbers. Toll-free numbers start with 900.

To call Spain from the U.S., dial 011-34 (international dial out and Spanish country code) and the nine-digit number.

To make an international call from Spain, dial 00, followed by the country code (1 for the United States and Canada), the area code (omitting the initial 0 if there is one), and the number. The easiest way to make a collect call is to dial 9900, then the country code, thus connecting you with an operator in the country you are calling.

**Spanish directory assistance** is 11888, while **international assistance** is 11825.

### Time Differences

From the last Sunday of October through the last Sunday of March, Barcelona is one hour ahead of Greenwich Mean Time; for the rest of the year (summer time) it is two hours ahead. If it's midnight in Barcelona, it is 6 p.m. on the same day in New York City and 3 p.m. in California.

### Tipping

Spain does not have a big tipping culture, but it's usual to leave a little cash (5 percent is quite sufficient) if service is not included. Locals leave change at bars *para el bote* (for the common tips fund). You can tip hotel porters and maids at the end of your visit.

### Travelers with Disabilities

Barcelona is improving quickly for wheelchair-bound visitors, who in general will still need to be accompanied. Only line 2 of the metro has elevator access to all stations, along with a few stations on other lines. This situation is being improved and all lines should be accessible soon. An increasing number of buses are adapted to the needs of the disabled. You can book specially adapted taxis by calling **Fono Taxi** *(933 001 100)*. A good website on the subject of travel in Barcelona is *www.accessiblebarcelona.com*.

## VISITOR INFORMATION

### Useful Websites

Turisme de Barcelona *(www.barcelonaturisme.com)* is the city's official tourist office site. The site of the Ajuntament de Barcelona, the city's town hall *(www.bcn.cat)*, contains interesting information on the city, including maps.

### Tourist Offices

**Oficina d'Informació de Turisme de Barcelona** (main city tourist office), Plaça de Catalunya, 17-S (underground), 08002, 932 853 832. Metro: Catalunya. Open daily 9 a.m.– 9 p.m. There are other tourist offices at Estació Sants train station and the airport. There is also a nationwide general tourist information service *(901 300 600)*.

## EMERGENCIES

### Consulates

■ **Canadian Consulate,** Carrer d'Elisenda de Pinós, 10, 932 042 700
■ **United Kingdom Consulate,** Avinguda Diagonal, 477, 933 666 200
■ **United States Consulate,** Passeig de la Reina Elisenda de Montcada, 23–25, 932 802 227

### Emergency Phone Numbers

General emergencies (all services), 112
■ Guàrdia Urbana (local police), 092
■ Policía Nacional (national police), 091
■ Guardia Civil (national military police, highway patrol, and other tasks), 062
■ Mossos d'Esquadra (regional Catalan police force that has taken over many duties of the Policía Nacional and Guardia Civil), 088
■ Fire, 080
■ Ambulance, 061
■ Hospital de la Santa Creu i de Sant Pau, Carrer de Sant Antoni Maria Claret, 167, 932 919 000
■ Hospital Clínic i Provincial, Carrer de Villarroel, 170, 932 775 400

There are 24-hour pharmacies at Carrer d'Aribau, 62 and Passeig de Gràcia, 26. Other pharmacies alternate on long shifts (9 a.m.–10 p.m.). Signs indicating the nearest one are posted at closed pharmacies, or you can get the day's list in *El País*.

### Lost Property

**Objetos perdidos (Ajuntament),** Carrer de la Ciutat, 9, 010. Open Mon.–Fri. 9 a.m.–2 p.m. If you leave anything in a taxi, call 902 101 564. In the case of things lost on the metro, try the Centre d'Atenció al Client at the Universitat stop, 933 187 074. Airport lost and found, 932 983 349.

# HOTELS

As long as Barcelona remains the flavor of the month for many travelers in Europe, you can expect competition for rooms to be tough. It is essential to make reservations as far ahead as possible. Barcelona is a fairly compact city, so you should be able to find a hotel within a reasonable distance of the sights. Remember that the city is a major destination for its nightlife, and Spaniards traditionally stay out long into the night, so you may prefer a room facing away from main roads. Many hotels accept all major cards, although *pensiones* (small family-run hotels) frequently do not take them at all.

TRAVEL ESSENTIALS

Hotels in Barcelona have multiplied over the past years to meet demand, which has taken some of the pressure off when looking for a room. Nevertheless, reservations are a good idea, and many hotels will require an acceptable credit card number to hold a room for you. The abbreviations used for credit cards are: AE (American Express), DC (Diners Club), MC (MasterCard), V (Visa). If you reserve too late, you may only find lodgings a long way from the center.

The hotel building boom has taken some of the upward pressure off room prices, too. For many years, inflation was crazy, but it has slowed. Lodging in Barcelona remains cheaper than in many major European cities.

The wave of hotel building has led to a proliferation of charming and boutique hotels, filling a prior gap in the market. Otherwise, there are plenty of comfortable could-be-anywhere places. We have also included a handful of the better *pensiones* for those looking for good but modest lodgings with a family touch. Rooms may come without

private baths—the prices listed here are for those with bathrooms en suite.

Barcelona is one of the noisiest cities in Europe, but many hotels have off-street rooms where the racket is greatly reduced, and double-glazing and air-conditioning can help. Those who are disturbed by noise should consider bringing earplugs.

Street parking is never easy to find in Barcelona and virtually impossible in the oldest parts of the city (where many streets are pedestrian-only). Many of the better hotels have limited garage space, but in some cases the garage is not actually on hotel property but close by. Most hotels are reasonably close to public parking, however. If you plan to have a vehicle, ask about parking when making your reservation.

**Grading System:** Hotels in Spain are officially categorized by the Generalitat into three divisions: Hotels and Hotel-Residencias, Hostals and Hostal-Residencias, and Pensiones. Stars are awarded within each division according

to different criteria, so a two-star hotel in the Hotel category is quite different from a two-star Pension.

Hotels (H) and Hotel-Residencias (HR) are awarded between one and five stars, depending on the number of rooms with full private bathrooms, TV, air-conditioning, and other facilities they have. Rooms in the hotels listed here have their own bathroom unless otherwise noted.

Hostals (HS) and Hostal-Residencias (HSR) tend to be more modest, and may be family run. Stars range from one to three. Pensiones (P) get one or two stars and are generally the simplest of establishments; you'll see plenty of these around.

The official star-rating system is not a particularly reliable guide to quality, and room rates are not regulated according to star ratings. Many hotels opt to stay in a lower category for tax purposes. Prices include sales tax (IVA) and in some cases continental or buffet breakfast (which is often compulsory).

## Price Ranges

An indication of the cost of a double room in the high season is given by € signs.

€€€€€  More than €300
€€€€  €220–€300
€€€  €150–€220
€€  €100–€150
€  Less than €100

## Text Symbols

**▪** No. of Guest Rooms
**▪** Public Transportation **P** Parking
**▪** Elevator **▪** Air-conditioning
**▪** Nonsmoking **▪** Outdoor Pool
**▪** Indoor Pool **▪** Health Club
**▪** Credit Cards

## Organization

Hotels listed here have been grouped first according to neighborhood, then listed alphabetically by price range.

# BARRI GÒTIC

During the day, the epicenter of Barcelona overflows with people, both locals and tourists. At night parts of it become quiet, while others hum with the activity of restaurants and bars. As in other areas of the old city, you need to be aware that some streets are potentially risky during the hours of darkness.

## ▪ HOTEL 1898
€€€€€ *****
LA RAMBLA, 109, 08002
TEL 935 529 552
FAX 935 529 550
www.hotel1898.com
Right in the action of La Rambla stands this graceful old building that in colonial days

was the seat of the Philippines Tobacco Company. Attentive service is a hallmark of this place, where rooms vary in size but have plenty of modern comforts. Furniture is tasteful and the rainfall showerheads a dream. Some suites have private indoor pools.

**▪** 169 **▪** Metro: Línia 3 (Liceu)
**P ▪ ▪ ▪ ▪ ▪**
**▪** All major cards

## ▪ COLÓN
€€€€ ****
AVINGUDA DE LA CATEDRAL, 7, 08002
TEL 933 011 404
FAX 933 172 915
www.colonhotelbarcelona.com
This is perhaps the choice hotel in the Barri Gòtic. The views alone, which extend across the square to the Catedral, are worth the cost. If you are fortunate enough to get one of the top-floor rooms with a terrace, you will be in heaven. However, if you end up with one of the back rooms you'll be looking onto nothing much at all. Decor varies from room to room.

**▪** 146 **▪** Metro: Línia 4 (Jaume I)
**P ▪ ▪** All major cards

## ▪ NERI
€€€€ ****
CARRER DE SANT SEVER, 5, 08002
TEL 933 040 655
FAX 933 040 337
www.hotelneri.com
Broad stone arches, carefully chosen timber furnishings, and the latest in design touches (like flat-screen plasma TVs) make this a stunning central option in a centuries-old mansion. Each room offers

an individual color scheme and decor. Have a relaxing snooze on the sundeck when sightseeing becomes too much.

**▪** 22 **▪** Metro: Línia 3 (Liceu)
**▪ ▪ ▪** All major cards

## ▪ SUIZO
€€€ ***
PLAÇA DE L'ÀNGEL, 12, 08002
TEL 933 106 108
FAX 933 105 0461
www.gargallo-hotels.com
Despite the aging exterior, this hotel has modern rooms that are simply and elegantly decorated. The common areas have a touch of old-world charm that is lacking in many more recently built hotels. An impressive buffet breakfast is served.

**▪** 50 **▪** Metro: Línia 4 (Jaume I)
**▪ ▪** All major cards

## ▪ JARDÍ
€€ *
PLAÇA DE SANT JOSEP ORIOL, 1, 08002
TEL 933 015 900
FAX 933 183 664
www.eljardi-barcelona.com
The front rooms in this delightfully located hotel make it a popular spot. If street noise bothers you, try to get a room off the square.

**▪** 40 **▪** Metro: Línia 3 (Liceu)
**▪ ▪** All major cards

## ▪ LEVANTE
€ *
BAIXADA DE SANT MIQUEL, 2, 08002
TEL 933 179 565
FAX 933 170 526
www.hostallevante.com
This old area is littered with hostels and cheap hotels, but

this is one of the brighter ones. A great range of rooms of varying size and quality are available. If a little street noise doesn't bother you, the doubles with balconies are the best.

**1** 50 **Metro**: Línia 3 (Liceu) **All major cards**

## LA RAMBLA & EL RAVAL

Barcelona's most famous boulevard is lined with hotels ranging from cheap student dives through some century-old stalwarts to the modern comforts of places like Le Meridien. A couple of good places can be found inside El Raval, too.

### ■ LE MERIDIEN
€€€€€ ****
LA RAMBLA, 111, 08002
TEL 933 186 200
FAX 933 017 776
**www.starwoodhotels.com**
One of the best addresses along La Rambla, Le Meridien has managed to hold its own against tough new competition. The rooms are luxurious and have rainfall showerheads and in-house movies for those who need a break from sightseeing.

**1** 233 **Metro**: Línia 3 (Catalunya or Liceu) **P** **All major cards**

### ■ CASA CAMPER
€€€€ ****
CARRER D'ELISABETS, 11, 08001
TEL 933 426 280
FAX 933 427 563
**www.casacamper.es**

This eccentric boutique stop has an intriguing room setup: On one side of a corridor are your sleeping quarters, while on the other side is your sitting room, complete with a hammock if sitting seems too strenuous. Furniture is rigorously designer hip, from the local style mecca Vinçon.

**1** 25 **Metro**: Línia 3 (Liceu) **All major cards**

### ■ SANT AGUSTÍ
€€€ ***
PLAÇA DE SANT AGUSTÍ, 3, 08001
TEL 933 181 658
FAX 933 172 928
**www.hotelsa.com**
Located just off La Rambla on a pleasant square, the hotel has been refurbished a couple of times and offers comfortable, understated, but modernized rooms, most with views across the square.

**1** 75 **Metro**: Línia 3 (Liceu) **All major cards**

### ■ MESÓN CASTILLA
€€ **
CARRER DE VALLDONZELLA, 5, 08001
TEL 933 182 182
FAX 934 124 020
**www.husa.es**
*Modernisme* creeps into the interior decoration in Mesón Castilla, particularly in the stained glass and murals in the public areas. The rooms are cozily decorated, and the location is comparatively quiet. Enjoy a relaxed breakfast in a room that looks out across an interior courtyard.

**1** 56 **Metro**: Línies 1 & 2 (Universitat) **P** **All major cards**

### ■ CONTINENTAL
€–€€ ***
LA RAMBLA, 138, 08002
TEL 933 012 570
FAX 933 027 360
**www.hotelcontinental.com**
One of Barcelona's once grand hotels, the Continental offers a touch of old-world charm at low rates. Try for rooms overlooking La Rambla. All have a refrigerator and microwave.

**1** 35 **Metro**: Línies 1, 2, & 3 (Catalunya) **All major cards**

### ■ HOTEL PENINSULAR
€ *
CARRER DE SANT PAU, 34, 08001
TEL 933 023 138
FAX 934 123 699
**www.hotelpeninsular.net**
In business as a hotel since the 1880s, this place was once a monastery. The rooms were monk's cells, and indeed they remain rather simple affairs to this day. They are, however, moderately priced, and the location sets you in the heart of the action, barely a leap from La Rambla. The plant-filled atrium is the hotel's calling card.

**1** 59 **Metro**: Línia 3 (Liceu) **All major cards**

## THE WATERFRONT

Several sleeping options occupy prime locations along the waterfront, and more are being built. A cluster of high-rise hotels concentrates in El Fòrum, and a sprinkling of hotels line the area that extends from there around the harbor toward Port Vell.

### ■ GRAND MARINA
**€€€€€ \*\*\*\***
**MOLL DE BARCELONA S/N, 08039**
**TEL 936 039 000**
**FAX 936 039 090**
**www.grandmarinahotel.com**
Occupying the landward flank of the portside World Trade Center, this hotel is situated in a splendid part of the city. Rooms are all generous in size, but the best are those on the wings with sea views. Timber, with a definite seaside flavor, dominates the decoration in the guest rooms and sunny public areas.
**[i]** 235 **[m]** *Metro: Línia 3 (Drassanes)* **P** 🔄 🔒 🏊 🚻
🔄 *All major cards*

### ■ HOTEL ARTS BARCELONA
**€€€€€ \*\*\*\*\***
**CARRER DE LA MARINA, 19–21, 08005**
**TEL 932 211 000**
**FAX 932 211 070**
**www.ritzcarlton.com**
For the international jet set, this is the address. Occupying 44 floors in one of the twin towers overlooking the Port Olímpic, Hotel Arts Barcelona oozes luxury and has stunning views. Sculpture, paintings, and palms are all part of the interior decoration.
**[i]** 455 **[m]** *Metro: Línia 4 (Ciutadella Vila Olímpica)*
**P** 🔄 🔒 🏊 🚻
🔄 *All major cards*

### ■ HOTEL 54
**€€€ \*\***
**PASSEIG JOAN DE BORBÓ, 54, 08003**
**TEL 932 250 054**
**FAX 932 250 080**
**www.hotel54barceloneta.es**

You'll have fun adjusting the color of room lighting here in this streamlined modern place. Rooms are otherwise fairly functional, but many have views over the port (go for these!). If you find yourself with a back room, you can always sit up on the roof terrace to watch the sunsets.
**[i]** 28 **[m]** *Metro: Línia 4 (Barceloneta)* 🔄 🔒
🔄 *All major cards*

### ■ HESPERIA DEL MAR HOTEL
**€€ \*\*\*\***
**CARRER DE ESPRONCEDA, 6, 08005**
**TEL 935 029 700**
**FAX 935 029 701**
**www.hesperia.com**
This businesslike hotel, spread over a half-dozen floors, is set back from the waterfront and occupies one of the better locations for city beaches. Rooms are of a reasonable size, with parquet floors, broad double beds, and, in many cases, a balcony from which you generally have at least a glimpse of the sea.
**[i]** 84 **[m]** *Metro: Línia 4 (Poblenou)* **P** 🔄 🔒
🔄 *All major cards*

### ■ HOTEL DEL MAR
**€€ \*\*\***
**PLA DE PALAU, 19, 08003**
**TEL 933 193 302**
**FAX 933 193 047**
**www.hoteldelmarbarcelona .com**
Set in a restrained, historic building, the modern rooms of the Hotel del Mar are best above all for the location. Here you are within a few

minutes' walk of the marina and Port Vell, the beaches and back lane restaurants of La Barceloneta, and the nightlife buzz of El Born. Some of the best rooms have balconies.
**[i]** 72 **[m]** *Metro: Línia 4 (Barceloneta)* 🔄 🔒 🔄
*All major cards*

## LA RIBERA

In the course of the 1990s, the area around the Born was rejuvenated. Given all this activity, the number of hotel options is limited, but growing. Along Via Laietana especially, a crop of upper-level hotels have been created.

### ■ CHIC & BASIC
**€€–€€€ \*\*\***
**CARRER DE LA PRINCESA, 50, 08003**
**TEL 932 954 652**
**FAX 932 954 653**
**www.chicandbasic.com**
The huge door to this high-ceilinged corner building almost looks forbidding. Within is revealed a dazzling design where white is the dominant color. Beds are grand (as is the central marble staircase!) and super comfortable, and some features of the old building have been retained.
**[i]** 31 **[m]** *Metro: Línia 4 (Jaume I)* 🔒 🔄 *All major cards*

### ■ BANYS ORIENTALS
**€€ \*\*\***
**CARRER DE L'ARGENTERIA, 37, 08003**
**TEL 932 688 460**
**FAX 932 688 461**
**www.hotelbanysorientals.com**

The best things come in small packages. Dominated by cool colors (sky and steel blue), timber details, and clean lines, this is a fine boutique option on a busy pedestrian street that's a two-minute walk away from the Església de Santa Maria del Mar. Rooms are smallish, but ooze a stylish charm.

ⓘ *43* 🚇 *Metro: Línia 4 (Jaume I)* 🔁 💲
💳 *All major cards*

### ■ GRAND HOTEL CENTRAL
€€
**VIA LAIETANA, 30, 08003**
**TEL 932 957 900**
**FAX 932 681 215**
**www.grandhotelcentral.com**
Stylish designer rooms, none smaller than 25 square yards (21 sq m) inside a proud-looking 1930s edifice, attract a fashionable clientele. Colors are muted and soothing, and rooms come with MP3 players. Another big draw is the rooftop pool with a sundeck and plenty of lounge space for those quiet moments.

ⓘ *147* 🚇 *Metro: Línia 4 (Jaume I)*
🔁 💲 🏊 🖥
💳 *All major cards*

## PASSEIG DE GRÀCIA

Not surprisingly, for this, the chic heart of central Barcelona, there is no shortage of quality hotels along the main boulevards. But also, there are some wonderful little surprises awaiting discovery in the narrow, fashionable streets of Gràcia.

### ■ CASA FUSTER
€€€€€ *****
**PASSEIG DE GRÀCIA, 132, 08008**
**TEL 932 553 000**
**FAX 932 553 002**
**www.hotelescenter.es**
It's hard to believe that this remarkable *modernista* edifice was once a bank. Renovated as a luxury hotel in 2004, it occupies a privileged spot at the northwestern end of Passeig de Gràcia. Take in the views from the roof. Modern, comfortable rooms are complemented by sumptuous public spaces.

ⓘ *105* 🚇 *Metro: Línies 3 e 5 (Diagonal)* 🅿 🔁 🏊 🖥
💳 *All major cards*

### ■ CLARIS
€€€€€ *****
**CARRER DE PAU CLARIS, 150, 08009**
**TEL 934 876 262**
**FAX 932 157 970**
**www.hotelclaris.com**
One of the city's top hotels, the Claris is known for its modern design and considerable art collection. The rooms cover a range of decoration from classic to some quite daring color combinations. Roman statues and Egyptian artifacts are sprinkled about. The rooftop bar is a stylish retreat.

ⓘ *124* 🚇 *Metro: Línies 2, 3, e 4 (Passeig de Gràcia)*
🅿 🏊 🖥 💳 *All major cards*

### ■ HOTEL MURMURI
€€€€ ****
**LA RAMBLA DE CATALUNYA, 104, 08008**
**TEL 935 500 600**
**FAX 935 500 601**
**www.murmuri.com**
Splendidly located at the northwestern end of a

leafy shopping boulevard in L'Eixample, this new hotel offers large rooms with a modern feel and gadgets like iPod adapters and Molton Brown bath products. The lobby bar is an agreeable spot to meet up with friends.

ⓘ *53* 🚇 *Metro: Línies 3 e 5 (Diagonal)* 🔁 💲 💲
💳 *All major cards*

### ■ MAJÈSTIC
€€€€€ *****
**PASSEIG DE GRÀCIA, 68, 08007**
**TEL 934 881 717**
**FAX 934 881 880**
**www.hotelmajestic.es**
This labyrinthine hotel's plush, elegantly appointed rooms are huge. A bright, modern design combines with ageless style. Discreetly placed item of statuary and works of art throughout public areas heighten the sense of class.

ⓘ *301* 🚇 *Metro: Línies 2, 3, e 4 (Passeig de Gràcia)*
🅿 💲 🏊 💳 *All major cards*

### ■ OMM
€€€€€ *****
**CARRER DE ROSELLÓ, 265, 08008**
**TEL 934 454 000**
**FAX 934 454 004**
**www.hotelomm.es**
One of the most self-conscious designer destinations in Barcelona, Omm is easily one of the most exciting options in town. It provides a feast of modern style, with ultramodern rooms lurking behind windows that seem to peel back from the metallic sheen of the facade.

ⓘ *59* 🚇 *Metro: Línies 3 e 5 (Diagonal)* 🔁 💲 🏊
💳 *All major cards*

### ■ HOTEL SIXTYTWO
€€€€€ ****
**PASSEIG DE GRÀCIA, 62, 08007**
**TEL 932 724 180**
**FAX 932 724 181**
**www.sixtytwohotel.com**
The steel-framed entrance is inserted into the 1930s facade, which is about all that remains of the original building. Inside is a stylish 21st-century design. Relax in the Zeroom with its library or in the Oriental garden out back. Rooms are sober and clean-lined with touches like Bang & Olufsen TVs.

**(1)** *45* **📷** *Metro: Línies 2, 3, & 4 (Passeig de Gràcia)*
**P 🅿 📺 ⛲** *All major cards*

### ■ AXEL
€€€€ ****
**CARRER D'ARIBAU, 33, 08011**
**TEL 933 239 393**
**FAX 933 239 394**
**www.axelhotels.com**
A top-of-the-line, gay-friendly hotel in the heart of Barcelona's gay quarter, the Axel hotel is a mix of stylish, century-old architecture and modern touches. The best rooms boast charming, sunny galleries. After a day's sightseeing, chill out with a cocktail in the rooftop Skybar and watch the sunset.

**(1)** *66* **📷** *Metro: Línies 1 & 2 (Universitat)* **🅿 🅿 ⛲ 📺**
**⛲** *All major cards*

### ■ HOTEL CONDES DE BARCELONA
€€€€ ****
**PASSEIG DE GRÀCIA, 73–75, 08008**
**TEL 934 450 000**
**FAX 934 453 232**
**www.condesdebarcelona.com**

Occupying two buildings facing each other across Carrer de Mallorca, this is an elegant option. If you can, try to reserve a room in the older of the two buildings, the stylishly remodeled Casa Enric Batlló. But, in either building, you will be able to bathe in marble luxury.

**(1)** *74* **📷** *Metro: Línies 2, 3, & 4 (Passeig de Gràcia)*
**P 🅿 🅿 ⛲** *All major cards*

### ■ ST. MORITZ
€€€€ ****
**CARRER DE LA DIPUTACIÓ, 264, 08007**
**TEL 934 121 500**
**FAX 934 121 236**
**www.hcchotels.es**
The spacious rooms (each with a marble bath) in this fine L'Eixample building are a pleasure to stay in. A relaxing place for a drink is the terrace-garden bar. For a little more exertion, try the small gym.

**(1)** *91* **📷** *Metro: Línies 2, 3, & 4 (Passeig de Gràcia)*
**P 🅿 📺 ⛲** *All major cards*

### ■ ASTORIA
€€€ ***
**CARRER DE PARÍS, 203, 08036**
**TEL 932 098 311**
**FAX 932 023 008**
**www.derbyhotels.com**
The Astoria is well located in a classic pre-Civil War building that is just a short walk from the top end of Passeig de Gràcia. This nicely renovated hotel has good-size, comfortable rooms.

**(1)** *117* **📷** *Metro: Línia 3 (Diagonal)* **P 🅿 🅿 ⛲ 📺**
**⛲** *All major cards*

### ■ BALMES
€€€ ***
**CARRER DE MALLORCA, 216, 08008**
**TEL 934 511 914**
**FAX 934 510 049**
**www.derbyhotels.com**
The crisp white brick of this modern and pleasing hotel sets the tone. Rooms are of average size with agreeable tiled bathrooms, and you have the option of lounging in the peaceful internal courtyard pool or the cozy garden.

**(1)** *100* **📷** *Metro: Línia 3 (Diagonal); FGC: Provença*
**P 🅿 🅿 ⛲** *All major cards*

### ■ GOYA
€€ *
**CARRER DE PAU CLARIS, 74, 08010**
**TEL 933 022 565**
**FAX 934 120 435**
**www.hostalgoya.com**
This quiet, family-run hostel is located on one of the most stylish streets in central Barcelona. From here, it is a quick walk into the Barri Gòtic and to La Pedrera. Try to reserve one of the renovated rooms, that are decorated with warm parquet floors.

**(1)** *19* **📷** *Metro: Línies 2, 3, & 4 (Universitat)* **🅿 🅿**
**⛲** *All major cards*

### ■ HOTEL CONSTANZA
€€ **
**CARRER DEL BRUC, 33, 08010**
**TEL 932 701 910**
**FAX 933 174 024**
**www.hotelconstanza.com**
The welcome is warm at this homey little boutique location that attracts plenty of attention from visitors on modest budgets. An unabashed

color scheme enlivens the impeccably maintained rooms. For a little more outlay, you could try a larger suite.

**①** 14 🚇 Metro: Línia 4 (Girona)
🔁 🅿 💳 All major cards

## LA SAGRADA FAMÍLIA TO PARK GÜELL

There are only a few hotels of note in the area around the two Gaudí sensations.

### ■ HISPANOS SIETE SUIZA
€€€ ***
**CARRER DE SICILIA, 255, 08025**
**TEL 932 082 051**
**FAX 932 082 052**
**www.hispanos7suiza.com**
The vintage cars that adorn the ground floor of this unique option set the scene. A brisk walk from La Sagrada Família and with its own fine restaurant, this home away from home offers apartment-size rooms with kitchens that can accommodate at least four guests. Each room has a terrace with a view.

**①** 19 🚇 Metro: Línies 2 & 5 (Sagrada Família) 🅿 🔁 🅿 💳 All major cards

### ■ CASA DOVER
€
**CÒRSEGA, 429, PRAL.1ª, 08037**
**TEL +34 672 250 387 (CELL)**
**www.casadover.com**
Within easy walking distance of two Gaudí monuments—La Sagrada Família and La Pedrera —this boutique bed and breakfast makes a good option. Modern furniture and subtle decor in its seven rooms give a stylish edge contrasting

with the building's classical facade. Also, it is in a great location on the edge of Gràcia, a bustling neighborhood with multiple dining choices.

**①** 7 🚇 Metro: Línia 4 (Verdaguer)
💳 Major cards except AE & DC

## CAMP NOU TO TIBIDABO

Big, comfortable, but often characterless hotels dot the broad Avinguda Diagonal between the city outskirts and the city's heart. But more personal options can be found in streets off the beaten path.

### ■ REY JUAN CARLOS I
€€€€€ *****
**AVINGUDA DIAGONAL, 661–671, 08028**
**TEL 933 644 040**
**FAX 933 644 264**
**www.hrjuancarlos.com**
On the edge of the city, this place is a businessmen's high-rise luxury establishment. Rooms are gathered around open glass galleries that look out over the city or into the central foyer.

**①** 419 🚇 Metro: Línia 3 (Zona Universitària); bus: 67 & 68
🅿 🔁 🅿 ♨ 🏊 🍽
💳 All major cards

### ■ ABAC
€€€€ *****
**AVINGUDA TIBIDABO, 1, 08022**
**TEL 933 196 600**
**FAX 933 196 601**
**www.abacbarcelona.com**
Located in a historic house with a garden in one of the most exclusive avenues on the hill leading up to Tibidabo,

this hotel oozes luxury from its most standard room to the Grand Suite, and from its soothing spa to the Michelin star award-winning restaurant.

**①** 15 🚇 Train: Avinguda Tibidao
🔁 🅿 💳 All major cards

## MONTJUÏC

At the foot of this Olympic hill, known for its museums, pretty landscaped gardens, and sports facilities, there are several functional hotels along Paral·lel and Plaça Espanya providing accommodation to people attending trade fairs. However, a recent renovation to former television studios has supplied the hill with a unique hotel in an exclusive location.

### ■ MIRAMAR
€€€€€ *****
**PLAÇA CARLOS IBÁÑEZ, 3, 08038**
**TEL 932 811 600**
**FAX 932 811 601**
**www.hotelmiramarbarcelona .es**
In a stunning position on the edge of the hill of Montjuïc looking over the port, all the rooms come with views and most have their own private terrace. After visiting the many cultural sites dotted all over Montjuïc, wallow in your Phillipe Starck bath or lounge on the teak surround of the slick outdoor pool. It also has a year-round indoor pool.

**①** 75 🚇 Metro: Línies 2 & 3 (Paral·lel) plus funicular (or taxi)
🅿 🔁 🅿 ♨ 🏊 🍽
💳 All major cards

TRAVEL ESSENTIALS

# LANGUAGE **GUIDE**

Barcelona is a bilingual city. Visitors with a reasonable grasp of Spanish will soon learn to distinguish it from the local tongue, Catalan (although some words are the same). Signs, menus, and so on increasingly appear exclusively in Catalan, so the following language guide and menu reader are given in Catalan/Spanish.

## Useful Words & Phrases

**Yes** *si/sí*
**No** *no*
**Excuse me** *perdoni/perdone*
**Hello** (before lunch) *bon dia!/ buenos días!*, (after lunch) *bona tarda!/¡buenas tardes!*
**Hi** *hola!/¡hola!*
**Please** *si us plau/por favor*
**Thank you** *gràcies/gracias*
**You're welcome** *de res/de nada*
**OK** *d'acord/de acuerdo*
**Goodbye** *adéu/adiós*
**Good night** *bona nit/buenas noches*
**Sorry** *ho sento/lo siento*
**Here** *aquí/aquí*
**There** *allà/allí*
**Today** *avui/hoy*
**Yesterday** *ahir/ayer*
**Tomorrow** *demà/mañana*
**Now** *ara/ahora*
**Later** *més tard/más tarde*
**This morning** *aquest matí/ esta mañana*
**This afternoon** *aquesta tarda/ esta tarde*
**This evening** *aquest vespre* or *aquesta nit/esta noche*
**Open** *obert/abierto*
**Closed** *tancat/cerrado*
**Do you speak English?** *¿Parla anglès?/¿Habla inglés?*
**I'd like...** *Voldria.../Quisiera*

**I don't understand** *No entenc/No entiendo*
**Please speak more slowly** *Si us plau, parli més a poc a poc/ Por favor, hable más despacio*
**Where is...?** *¿On és...?/¿Donde está...?*
**What is your name?** *¿Com es diu?/¿Cómo se llama?*
**My name is...** *Em dic.../Me llamo...*
**At what time?** *¿A quina hora?/¿A qué hora?*
**When?** *¿Quan?/¿Cuándo?*
**Can you help me?** *¿Em pot ajudar?/¿Me puede ayudar?*
**How much is it?** *¿Quant costa?/¿Cuánto vale?*

## Menu Reader

**breakfast** *l'esmorzar/ el desayuno*
**lunch** *el dinar (el menjar)/ el almuerzo (la comida)*
**dinner** *el sopar/la cena*
**appetizer** *l'entrant/el entrante*
**first course** *el primer/ el primero*
**main course** *el segon/ el segundo*
**vegetable, side dish** *la guarnició/la guarnición*
**dessert** *les postres/el postre*
**menu** *la carta*
**wine list** *la carta de vins/ la carta de vinos*
**the check** *el compte/la cuenta*
**I'd like to order** *Ja pot prendre nota/Ya puede tomar nota*

## Drinks (Begudes/Bebidas)
**water** *aigua/agua*
**orange juice** *suc de taronja/ zumo de naranja*
**beer** *cervesa/cerveza*
**white wine** *vi blanc/vino blanco*

**red wine** *vi negre/vino tinto*
**coffee** *cafè/café*
**short black coffee** *cafè sol*
**tea** *tè/té*
**with milk** *amb llet/con leche*

### Meat *(Carn/Carne)*
*ànec/pato* **duck**
*anyell/cordero* **lamb**
*bistec* **beefsteak**
*bou/buey* **bull (beef)**
*conill/conejo* **rabbit**
*pernil/jamón* **ham**
*porc/cerdo* **pork**
*pollastre/pollo* **chicken**
*salsitxa/salsicha* **sausage**
*vedella/ternera* **veal**

### Seafood *(Mariscos)*
*bacallà/bacalao* **salted cod**
*cloïsses/almejas* **clams**
*cranc/cangrejo* **crab**
*gambes/gambas* **prawns**
*llagosta/langosta* **lobster**
*lluç/merluza* **hake**
*musclos/mejillones* **mussels**
*ostres/ostras* **oysters**
*pop/pulpo* **octopus**
*tonyina/atún* or *bonito* **tuna**

### Vegetables *(Verdures/Verduras)*
*albergínia/berenjena* **eggplant**
*all/ajo* **garlic**
*amanida/ensalada* **salad**
*arròs/arroz* **rice**
*bolets/setas* **mushrooms**
*carxofa/alcachofa* **artichoke**
*ceba/cebolla* **onion**

### Fruit *(Fruites/Frutas)*
*cireres/cerezas* **cherries**
*maduixes/fresas* **strawberries**
*poma/manzana* **apple**
*préssec/melocotón* **peach**
*raïm/uva* **grapes**
*taronja/naranja* **orange**

# INDEX

INDEX

## Walking Barcelona

### Published by the National Geographic Society

John M. Fahey, Fr., *Charman of the Board and Chief Executive Officer*
Declan Moore, *Executive Vice President; President,*
*Publishing and Travel*
Melina Gerosa Bellows, *Executive Vice President; Publisher and*
*Chief Creative Officer, Books, Kids, and Family*
Lynn Cutter, *Executive Vice President, Travel*
Keith Bellows, *Senior Vice President and Editor in Chief, National*
*Geographic Travel Media*

### Prepared by the Book Division

Hector Sierra, *Senior Vice President and General Manager*
Janet Goldstein, *Senior Vice President and Editorial Director*
Jonathan Halling, *Creative Director*
Marianne R. Koszorus, *Design Director*
Barbara A. Noe, *Senior Editor, National Geographic Travel Books*
Elisa Gibson, *Designer*
R. Gary Colbert, *Production Director*
Mike Horenstein, *Production Manager*
Jennifer A. Thornton, *Director of Managing Editorial*
Meredith C. Wilcox, *Director, Administration and Rights Clearance*

### Production Services

Phillip L. Schlosser, *Senior Vice President*
Chris Brown, *Vice President, NG Book Manufacturing*
Robert L. Barr, *Manager*
Neal Edwards, *Imaging*

### Created by Toucan Books Ltd

Ellen Dupont, *Editorial Director*
Louise Tucker, *Editor*
Dave Jones, *Designer*
Alba Sinca, *Editorial Support*
Merritt Cartographic, *Maps*
Marion Dent, *Proofreader*
Marie Lorimer, *Indexer*

The information in this book has been carefully checked and to the best of our knowledge is accurate. However, details are subject to change, and the National Geographic Society cannot be responsible for such changes, or for errors or omissions. Assessments of sites, hotels, and restaurants are based on the author's subjective opinions, which do not necessarily reflect the publisher's opinion.

The National Geographic Society is one of the world's largest nonprofit scientific and educational organizations. Its mission is to inspire people to care about the planet. Founded in 1888, the Society is member supported and offers a community for members to get closer to explorers, connect with other members, and help make a difference. The Society reaches more than 450 million people worldwide each month through *National Geographic* and other magazines; National Geographic Channel; television documentaries; music; radio; films; books; DVDs; maps; exhibitions; live events; school publishing programs; interactive media; and merchandise. National Geographic reflects the world through its magazines, television programs, films, music and radio, books, DVDs, maps, exhibitions, live events, school publishing programs, interactive media and merchandise. National Geographic has fund more than 10,000 scientific research, conservation, and exploration projects and supports an education program promoting geography literacy. For more information, visit www.nationalgeographic.com.

For more information, please call 1-800-NGS LINE (647-5463) or write to the following address:

National Geographic Society
1145 17th Street N.W.
Washington, D.C. 20036-4688 U.S.A.

For information about special discounts for bulk purchases, please contact National Geographic Books Special Sales: ngspecsales@ngs.org

For rights or permissions inquiries, please contact National Geographic Books Subsidiary Rights: ngbookrights@ngs.org

ISBN: 978-1-4262-1271-0

Printed in Hong Kong
13/THK/1